"A powerful
-Nick Saban, 7-1

VICTORY OUTSIDE THE ARENA

How Athletes Can Go from Isolated to Inspired Once the Applause Begins to Fade

BILL BURKE

Copyright © 2024 by Bill Burke

All rights reserved.

ISBN: (Print) 979-8-9896937-0-2
ISBN: (eBook) 979-8-9896937-1-9

No portion of this book may be reproduced in any form without written permission from the publisher or author, except as permitted by U.S. copyright law.

This publication is designed to provide accurate and authoritative information about the subject matter covered. It is sold with the understanding that neither the author nor the publisher is engaged in rendering legal, investment, accounting, or other professional services. While the publisher and author have used their best efforts in preparing this book, they make no representations or warranties with respect to the accuracy or completeness of the contents of this book. The advice and strategies contained herein may not be suitable for your situation. You should consult with a professional when appropriate.

TIME OUT!

Thank you for picking up this book. I hope you find it helpful on your journey.

Since you've already proven your commitment to self-improvement, I'd like to offer you a free gift that can serve as a reminder of that commitment.

Get your copy of the *Former Athlete Fire Framework* here: **outsidethearena.com/framework**

Many thanks,
Bill Burke

DEDICATION

To my three anchors: Christina, Blake, and Brooklyn.

To my parents, who were the first to teach me to finish the drill.

To every athlete courageous enough to walk into the arena knowing that one day they'd have to walk out.

CONTENTS

INTRODUCTION — 1

PART ONE: FIERCE KNOWLEDGE — 11

CHAPTER 1: TRIAL BY FIRE — 15

CHAPTER 2: WHEN THE FLAME FLICKERS — 31

CHAPTER 3: THROUGH THE SMOKE — 47

PART TWO: INSPIRED INTENTION — 63

CHAPTER 4: MENTAL DYNAMITE — 67

CHAPTER 5: IGNITE YOUR INFLUENCE — 83

CHAPTER 6: THE BURNING QUESTION — 101

PART THREE: RELENTLESS ACTION — 119

CHAPTER 7: CREATE THE SPARK — 123

CHAPTER 8: FAN THE FLAMES — 137

CHAPTER 9: FEEL THE HEAT — 153

PART FOUR: EPIC FOCUS	**167**
CHAPTER 10: NO FRICTION, NO FIRE	171
CHAPTER 11: HARNESS THE BLAZE	185
CHAPTER 12: EXPLODE EXPECTATIONS	201
CONCLUSION: SEE THE LIGHT	217

INTRODUCTION

The phone on the nightstand next to my bed rang at 7:30 a.m., jolting me out of a deep sleep. Startled by the ear-piercing shrill of the phone, I shot up and tried to quickly figure out where I was.

Right. My Secaucus, New Jersey hotel room. The life of a player trying to make the 53-man roster in the NFL lends itself to a blur of dorm mattresses and extended-stay shared hotel rooms.

Without any scheduled activities until late that morning, I wasn't prepared to wake up that early—and I certainly wasn't prepared to hear the voice of the Director of Administration for the New York Football Giants, Jim Phelan, on the other end of the line. He didn't offer a "good morning" or any other pleasantries.

"Bill? I need you to head over to the stadium now. Bring your playbook."

All I could offer was an uninspired "Okay," and with that, he hung up. After all, he most likely had more players to call. But as I threw the blankets off my body, I couldn't help but notice that my roommate Adam Young, a tight end from Dartmouth University, hadn't received the same call as me. He'd get to continue sleeping and would remain on the team for at least another week.

I had gone undrafted out of college and did not have many NFL teams knocking down my door to sign me. The signing bonus I received was a meager one thousand dollars. That might sound like a nice sum of money to a broke college student, but the amount of a player's signing bonus indicated how much confidence the organization had in him. (Ron Dayne, the Giants' first draft pick that year, received a $4.5 million bonus to sign his contract.)

I guess the call shouldn't have come as a surprise, considering the few reps I'd had in practice and the fact that I hadn't gotten any playing time in the preseason games. I was holding out hope anyway. I was so consumed with trying to quickly learn the six-inch thick playbook that there wasn't room in my head for entertaining when the call might come.

Regardless of where he was picked, every player trying to make a roster in the most elite football organization on the planet knew what the phrase "bring your playbook" meant. You were done. You were being shown the door. "Bring your playbook" signified that you were being released.

I had reached my goal of making it to the NFL, but only as an undrafted free agent. I had been a long shot to make the team from the beginning of training camp, and now it seemed that this was the day when I'd have to face the harsh reality that, for the first time in my life, I wasn't good enough.

After arriving at the stadium, I met with Head Coach Jim Fassel for precisely three minutes and listened to his reasons for cutting me loose. After a few hollow but supportive words, I was given a handshake and a "good luck." Next stop: the airport and a one-way ticket back to Ohio.

I walked out of Fassel's office and slowly descended the staircase that led to the locker room. As I walked through the quiet and mostly empty locker room, I thought I'd grab my helmet or jersey to take with me as a keepsake, a reminder of how far I'd made it. But to my mild surprise, my locker had already been cleaned out. While I had been asleep in the hotel early that morning, the equipment staff for the team ensured that any evidence of me being a part of that team was wiped away. No jersey. No helmet. Even my nameplate had been removed to make room for the next man up.

Hearing that I wasn't good enough for the first time in my life was hard enough, but seeing my empty locker felt like a second punch in the face. You dream about the possibilities of being paid handsomely to play a kid's game and all the external accolades and status that come with the job, not to mention the thrill of competition and performing in front of raucous crowds.

But you never dream about the day you'll be told you can't be on the team. It was the very first time in my life that I was made to feel like I didn't belong, and it was a tough pill to swallow.

From the first time I saw a football game on TV at the age of 5 through the end of my playing career at 24, my identity and self-worth were tied to football. Everyone knew me as an athlete. That's where I fit in, and I was good at it. I was told I was talented, which gave me a sense of pride.

I continued to thrive every year until I received a full scholarship to play quarterback at Michigan State University for the now legendary coach Nick Saban. While there, I broke records, was a part of some of the greatest games in school history, and helped our team finish my senior season ranked seventh in the nation. I pursued the dream of playing the game for a living and spent an off-season with the New York Giants of the NFL.

But then, after a few more tryouts, it became apparent that my dream was dying fast and that a major chapter in my life was closing—without my permission.

You and I have never met, at least not yet. But I do know something about you already. You have a similar story to mine. The names, places, and circumstances vary somewhat, but the theme is the same: You played your final game. "There's always next season" is not a phrase that you will hear ever again. Game over. And with the end comes so many emotions, all swirling together.

You know on some level that you are experiencing a big loss in your life, but your forward-looking athlete brain is telling you that there's no time to grieve, no time to admit defeat. So you try to push forward. But push towards what? You feel an urgency to have it all figured out. People are looking to you to excel. You have certain internal expectations as well. But where can you apply them?

I had heard that the end would come, but never really let myself believe it. And it always felt like the people delivering that message didn't want to believe it either. Like it wouldn't be their problem. Although there was some level of sadness and disappointment after sixteen years of excitement and hope, the real problem was that I had no idea what to do next.

Where was the person who would tell me what the next step was? There always seemed to be no shortage of people wanting to help support the cultivation of my athletic progress. And if they didn't want to support it, they were at least interested in it. So where did everybody go? The problem was now mine to figure out.

As months bled into years, the frustration continued. I was unfulfilled. I was downright unhappy. And it began to feel like the universe was pushing back against me. I had always considered myself ambitious and hard-working with a desire to be successful. So why didn't I feel right? The answer slowly began to reveal itself: I wasn't growing, didn't know myself well outside of sports, and lacked clarity about what I wanted.

I wasn't actively putting in the necessary time and work to uncover why I couldn't seem to unstick myself and start moving in the direction of fulfillment. I was waiting for someone or something to point me in the right direction. Instead of being an active participant in discovering the full scope of my potential, I was watching from the sidelines.

Why hadn't I yet found something that lit me up like competitive athletics? Was there something wrong with me? Did I not have a strong work ethic? Why did I feel like I was treading water and going nowhere fast? Were my best days behind me? How did I get here? I realized something had to change.

INTRODUCTION

I knew, without question, that I could achieve great things outside of sports. But I didn't know how or what skills I needed. Football had been the only thing that I'd ever been passionate about. These questions had bubbled under the surface since my athletic career ended, and I assumed the answers would reveal themselves at some point. But as I would later discover, those answers are actually quite simple to find if you know what steps to take and are courageous enough to put in the work to pursue them.

Are you waiting? If so, are you *tired* of waiting? Have you had enough of feeling the complete opposite of how you felt as an athlete? As a player, when you were pushed to your limits, I'll bet your response was one of tenacity. I'd guess that you didn't hang your head for long after a setback. You didn't wait to get after it again. You couldn't wait.

The longer you delay, the more you avoid the big issues in your life, the greater the chance that you'll drift towards an ordinary life. You'll get what you are willing to accept. Most of our suffering comes from avoidance. Embrace the pain, but refuse to tolerate it.

During my time at Michigan State, every Monday, our head coach Nick Saban (who at the time of writing this book has won seven National Championships) would address the team and set the tone for the week. With a theme or anecdote, he would lay out what our mental approach should be or what we should be focused on.

On one particular Monday, I walked into the auditorium and was planted firmly in my seat five minutes before the scheduled start time of our team meeting. (I, along with most of my teammates, subscribed to the philosophy of "if you're on time, you're late." Being late to any function, even by a few seconds, was met with unpleasant consequences.)

Coach Saban started this meeting off with a question: "How long does a typical football play last?" Having played over a hundred organized football games in my life by that point, it was a question

5

that I had never considered. He quickly offered the answer. "The typical football play lasts for six seconds." He went on to say that six seconds is not a long time to do anything and while every play is a challenge, giving everything you have for that brief time is very achievable.

Then he asked us to imagine sticking our hands in a fire for six seconds. What would happen? It would, of course, be excruciating and most likely leave some scars. To endure that kind of pain, you would have to be fully committed to those six seconds. And when you think about it, all of that's true.

The game of football is hard. And while a play lasts only that short amount of time, what can occur during that time can feel like an eternity. Pain, strain, exhaustion, sweat, collision, fear, failure, distraction, noise, and doubt can happen simultaneously during those six seconds. None of it is comfortable. But when short bursts of intense effort are stacked on top of each other consistently, eventually, magical things can start to happen. Elation, euphoria, excitement, and ultimately, victory can be captured in those few seconds as well.

"Stick your hand in the fire" kept replaying in my head for years after I had walked off the Michigan State campus for the final time as a player. It has since become a motto as well as the framework for the transformation I've been through and for the athletes I talk with who continue to pursue it.

> **F**ierce Knowledge (of who we are today and what's possible in the future)
> **I**nspired Intention (a plan for what we want out of our lives)
> **R**elentless Action (dreams die without a process to achieve them)
> **E**pic Focus (shining a light on what matters most)

As a result of following this formula, I have achieved a greater perspective, am pursuing my purpose, have even more perseverance than I did when I was an athlete, have a deeper understanding of patience, and am at peace with who I am and who I'm becoming. I want the same for you.

If you choose to follow this process, you can have a life much more fulfilling than any athletic event could provide. The excitement and hope you will feel will be immeasurable. You will feel a confidence that even thousands of screaming fans chanting your name could not instill in you.

The best part? There's no last game or last season. No one can tell you that you can't play anymore. It's a game that you can play forever.

But don't make the same mistake I did. Don't wait for it to happen *to* you. If you think it will all work out on its own, chances are good that it won't. You may end up okay, with a paycheck, a place to live, and the necessities. But who wants to be just okay? Who wants to be average? That's not why you were put on earth. That's not why you were given the gifts you have. You want to be great, and you have greatness inside of you. It's incredible how much mediocrity is all around us. Don't bring yourself down to average, and don't spend well over a decade drifting as I did.

Do you want to know why you're feeling the way you are right now? Would you like an assist with processing the change and smoothing the transition? I'll help you shine a light on what's unique about you *without* your sport. You'll start seeing the unlimited possibilities for your future and be propelled forward by hope that there is something else out there just for you.

Do you want to know how the future can be brighter than the past? Do you want more, wish you could do more, give more, or be more? Are you feeling uncertain about your future? Are you experiencing hesitation and determination both at once? Take the challenging but rewarding steps to change the way you think and feel and the results you can achieve. It may be uncomfortable, you may squirm, and you will at times feel the urge to pull away.

There's a fantastic opportunity that exists for all of us. That opportunity is to chase down our dreams and live a life that leaves us feeling inspired. I want to look back and say that I "left it all on the field" in the game of life. If you feel the same way, I invite you to take the trip with me.

I challenge you to stick your hand in the fire.

A NOTE ON HOW TO READ THIS BOOK

At the end of each chapter, you'll find some STICK YOUR HAND IN THE FIRE questions. These are meant to push you to apply what you just read. It doesn't do you any good to just read the chapter, move on, and stay the same.

The book you've begun reading is designed to get you to reflect and act. I strongly encourage you to grab a notebook or journal (or open a blank document on your laptop) and *record* the answers to these end-of-chapter questions. Just like you put in the behind-the-scenes time on the field or court, investing the effort here will pay off as you find victory outside the arena.

F

Part One

FIERCE KNOWLEDGE

Tell me if you've heard this before: "Have a plan."

It sounds like good advice, right? Without a solid plan, you can't get where you want to go. After all, if you tried to climb Mt. Everest without first determining the route you would take up the mountain, the equipment you would need to bring, and when you'd stop to rest, you would probably fail almost instantly.

There is an important step that you need to take before embarking on any new expedition. Take the time and devote the energy to acquiring *fierce knowledge*.

What is fierce knowledge? It's crucial information you'll need to understand how you are feeling now. It's what you learned and experienced as an athlete and what that means for you now and in the future. Acquiring this knowledge will need to be attacked with a certain zeal and sense of urgency. The same fierce attitude that propelled you to success as an athlete will be required here too. Proactive, not passive. Necessary to have instead of nice to have. You will need to be proactive in seeking it out.

It's what you need to know to establish your plan. It's the starting point. It's the hard part. It's the crucial step that far too many athletes (and non-athletes as well) skip over. Too many of us plow ahead without assessing what just happened. You invested years into your athletic endeavors, why not take some time to process that experience to better prepare for what's next?

What's dangerous about knowing what you want and what you excel at from a young age is that you don't think to *reflect* on who you are. It doesn't seem necessary. You believe you already know. Or worse, you don't want to know.

One of the most fundamental aspects of being a competitive athlete is assessing the game or match you just played after it's over. You reflected on what you did well and what you could've done better. You analyzed yourself along with the help of coaches. You watched game film of yourself. And with that knowledge, you discovered how you could improve and move forward more confidently during the next game. Knowledge is power. Knowledge can make you better. Knowledge can take you from good to great. Knowledge can make you *dangerous*.

Attacking the next phase of life is no different. You don't need a plan just yet. What you need is information. You need to know and understand some things about what just happened, and more importantly, you need to begin to understand who you *are* (not just who you were.)

Taking time to understand how you feel and why can spark a deep level of curiosity and understanding of yourself. You will start paying attention to your thoughts and you'll begin to question why you are thinking them. This will equip you to move forward with more confidence.

This knowledge is acquired by asking yourself some very direct questions. I will be honest with you; these questions can be difficult to answer. You will need to give them the same time, devotion, and energy you gave to your sport. They mean that much to your future. Turning your attention immediately to what may be next for you would be to withhold the proper respect you owe yourself. I learned this one the hard way.

Regardless of what sport you played, for how long, and at what level, you were drawn to this world for very specific reasons. If you were like me, you probably didn't give those reasons much thought at the time. It just felt good to play. But now that it's over or coming to an end, it's time to take stock.

> *What was so special about being an athlete?*
> *What does the word "athlete" mean to you?*
> *How did being an athlete make you feel?*
> *Why did it matter to you?*
> *Now that it's over, what have you lost?*
> *How will you deal with the loss?*
> *Who are you now, without sports?*
> *Who were you before?*
> *What do you want?*
> *What are you really looking for?*

This is the knowledge we'll be digging into in the chapters to come. Let's get started.

"I firmly believe that any man's finest hour—his greatest fulfillment to all he holds dear—is that moment when he has worked his heart out in a good cause and lies exhausted on the field of battle, victorious."

—Vince Lombardi

1

TRIAL BY FIRE

None of the 76,895 fans left the stadium when the game ended. As I celebrated the victory by jumping up and down in unison with my teammates at midfield, I couldn't help but notice that most of the fans were not making their way toward the exits. Granted, most of those in attendance that day waited all week, planned elaborate tailgates, and were there to witness the home team Michigan State Spartans defeat the visiting, rival Michigan Wolverines. So when they got the result they were hoping for, they wanted to savor every moment. So did I.

It was one of those games I dreamt about playing as a kid. It was the kind of game that was so competitive and tense that it moved any observer closer to the edge of their seat every time the ball was snapped.

Some players from both teams had played against each other in high school, both teams were undefeated and wanted to remain that way, and an in-state rivalry where the two schools are only separated by sixty miles always stirs emotions. The state of Michigan is a state divided, with families that have alumni from both schools living in the same house. It was the type of game that left most fans, regardless of their allegiance to their favorite team, smiling because they knew they had just witnessed a closely contested battle. It was great entertainment.

It was the biggest game of my career. It was also easily the biggest game of our season. Michigan came into the game with a 5-0 record and ranked third in the country. Two years earlier, they had won the National Championship and were now led by a quarterback named Tom Brady. He wasn't yet the same player he is today, having won seven NFL Super Bowls, but I would see flashes of excellent play during our game. His accuracy on tight throws and calm confidence never allowed us to relax or become complacent.

On the other hand, we were also undefeated at 5-0 and ranked #11 in the nation. Not bad for a team that went 6-6 the year before and didn't even qualify for a bowl game. But our fans had seen this movie before. Just two years earlier, we had started the season undefeated, but when we met Michigan in the middle of the season, they handed us our first loss. Many fans wondered if this year's meeting would produce the same result.

To be honest, it's hard to not let the demons from the past taunt you as you think about how the game might play out. (And this is just as true of life after sports too.)

As if we needed more reminders of the stakes, ESPN was in town to broadcast College GameDay live from our campus in East Lansing. That show was and still is the biggest college football show in America, and they only traveled to the biggest game in the country every week. Camera crews were in our building throughout the week, filming our every move. This turned up the pressure just a bit, but the excitement was building as well. This level of attention and the feeling that I was performing on the biggest stage in the country was partly why I had always wanted to play at a big school.

Under an overcast sky, a temperature of 55 degrees, and a packed house, the scene in the stadium couldn't have been scripted any better. We started the game hot and were leading 34-17 early in the fourth quarter. After an admirable comeback led by Brady, Michigan pulled to within three points late in the game. As I stood on the sideline watching Brady calmly march his team down the field, I couldn't help but flash back to something Coach Saban had said to me in his office years earlier that drew from his time as a coach in the NFL. "Every game in the NFL comes down to the last two minutes."

So I wasn't shocked to see our lead slipping away. They had the momentum, and the only question was, *would they run out of time?* Our defense did its job yet again and gave us the ball back with the lead. The offense was tasked with putting the nail in the coffin.

After a pass to the sideline that enabled us to pick up a first down, the clock ran out. We held on to win 34-31. My teammates and I broke school records that day while overcoming the ghosts of several setbacks from the previous two years, individually and as a team. We had broken through.

Seven days later, though, a very different story played out. After beating Michigan, our national ranking had now jumped to #5. That number felt surreal. The pregame hype still attracted a national television audience, but everything else about our game with Purdue was different. We were going on the road to a foreign and unfriendly environment. Although the stadium on Purdue's campus wasn't the biggest in capacity, the layout positioned fans very close to the sidelines, where the players could feel the intensity of the environment. This increased the noise level of the stadium and added an extra layer of difficulty to an already enormous challenge.

When you are ranked fifth in the country and competing at that level of competition, your next opponent is not intimidated. It's actually quite the opposite. They can't wait to test themselves against one of the best teams in the country. From this point forward, we would get everyone's best shot. And on that day, our opponent came out swinging.

The quarterback for Purdue that day was another future Hall of Famer, Drew Brees. Not only was Brees a great player, but the offensive system they ran was extremely difficult on opposing defenses and tested their physical and mental toughness.

Playing on the road is always tough, but we were coming off an emotional win against our biggest rival. There had been a tremendous amount of buildup, and with that usually comes an emotional letdown. Those don't always translate into a loss on the field, but sustaining the same intensity and focus week in and week out is difficult. We would score first, but the game wasn't even close after that.

Contrary to my performance just one week earlier, this time I had played one of the worst games of my career. What a difference a week can make. As I watched the last seconds on the clock tick off, the emotions of the previous week seemed like an all-but-forgotten memory. I watched the other team celebrate on the field exactly as we had at the last game's conclusion. The expressions on their faces reflected what we had experienced a short time ago. The roles were reversed entirely. They had captured the win and sent us home with our heads down, wondering how one week we could be on top of the world and the next could feel like the end.

One of my least favorite parts of enduring a loss was walking out of the locker room. Fans and families were waiting to embrace the players and show support and encouragement. But the last thing I wanted to hear after a tough loss was "Good game." How could it be a good game if the outcome wasn't a win? And I definitely didn't want anyone's sympathy. What I wanted was another shot.

In the immediate aftermath of a loss, the physical and emotional wounds are still fresh, and it can be hard to put what just happened away into a nice little box and treat it as a unique experience. It's hard to have perspective.

But as time started to pass and the sting of the loss started to dissipate, I remember feeling an odd sense of satisfaction. I never really acknowledged it or analyzed it, but I felt something just under the surface.

It wasn't until many years after my career ended that I thought back to those times and wondered about exactly that feeling. Could it be that the naïveté of youth allowed me to shake off the low moments quickly? Or maybe it was the common 24-hour rule that most programs adhere to which stated that the celebration of a win or the despair of a loss had to be over within that short time frame. There was always more work to be done and another challenge that needed my attention.

Since my playing career ended, I've thought a lot about why I loved playing a game so much. I would become incredibly reflective when watching a football game with championship implications on the line, the games that mattered the most. Watching the post-game celebrations and interviews with the players and coaches, I could feel the emotion coming through the TV screen. The emotion of having been in the battle. The tears of joy and the tears of disappointment. The exhaustion of having given the cause everything they had. Obviously, the players and coaches that came out on top were thrilled that they had won—everyone loves to win—but there had to be more to it than that.

Athletes are the risk-takers. And despite all the risks, including physical injury and the much more damaging risk of not coming out of the contest as a winner, we play anyway. We walk into a place where we don't expect easy victories. The win against Michigan would've been great by any final score, but the fact that the final minutes were in doubt made the triumph even sweeter. It's more fulfilling to be able to walk off the field with a win and feel exhausted than with a win knowing it didn't require every bit of your soul to achieve it.

Athletes step into an arena because we aren't satisfied *dreaming* about the possibilities of what those moments might feel like. We need to *experience* it for ourselves. Every time we step inside the walls, there is a chance that we'll feel worse than when we walked in. And that choice takes a special type of nervous system.

There's a possibility that we'll have to watch our opponent celebrate as we agonize over what went wrong. The possible emotional outcomes sit at polar opposites of a very distinct and short spectrum. The elation that comes with triumph exceeds our dreams of what it will feel like when it happens. The pain of a defeat can be devastating and the only solace is a bit of satisfaction that comes from knowing there will be another opportunity to make it all right. Regardless of the outcome, athletes know it's better to be on the *inside* and lose than on the *outside* and not know.

THE MAN IN THE ARENA

Teddy Roosevelt, the 26th President of the United States, delivered a speech after his term ended that sums up what I felt during the highs and the lows of what appeared—on the surface—to be just a game. And he did it perfectly.

On April 23, 1910, in Paris, France, Roosevelt gave a talk titled *Citizenship In A Republic*. More commonly referred to as *The Man In The Arena* speech, it's a group of words that articulates precisely why I found satisfaction and fulfillment even in the most gut-wrenching losses. It best describes to me what I loved most about being an athlete. I've not been able to find a better description of what makes being an athlete so special. I feel fortunate to have experienced what these words describe. I know you do too.

> "It is not the critic who counts, not the one who points out how the strong man stumbled or how the doer of deeds might have done them better. The credit belongs to the man who is actually in the arena, whose face is marred with sweat and dust and blood; who strives valiantly; who errs and comes short again and again; who knows the great enthusiasms, the great devotions, and spends himself in a worthy cause; who, if he wins, knows the triumph of high achievement; and who, if he fails, at least fails while daring greatly, so that his place shall never be with those cold and timid souls who know neither victory nor defeat."

He was speaking about the state of America and its ever-changing place in the world. Still, it's amazing how his words reverberate through the athletic world and speak directly to those who competed in *actual* arenas.

The arenas that athletes like you and I step into are more than just places to have fun and compete. They are a sacred space reserved for those who want to test the edges of their own capabilities instead of wondering what the elation of victory could feel like. It's a place where there are multiple battles happening simultaneously.

There's the obvious battle against the player or team vying for the same things that you're after: the trophy, self-satisfaction, bragging rights. Then there's the more subtle and hidden opponent that you're up against—yourself. This is the much less discussed challenge but at the same time, it's the more fundamental reason you're there in the first place.

The tension, uncertainty, and anticipation that starts to brew inside your stomach hours before the contest haunt you and force questions that you've been trying to suppress to the surface. *Am I good enough? Do I have what it takes?* When the game ends and the answer to these is "Yes!", the feelings of euphoria are hard to match in any other place.

On the other hand, when you come up short of the glory, the emotional aftermath can torture you until the next opportunity arises. Either way, you know where you stand when the dust settles.

There's an allure to the clarity of knowing how you stacked up to your challenger. And to your own standards. Certain people are attracted to these arenas because they realize instinctively that they have more to offer than just the chance to win a game. They are drawn to the pursuit of overcoming the pain and uncertainty that stops most people from striving and reaching to morph into something more than they were the day before. The magic is in the doing, the experiencing, the ecstasy, the devastation, the wrestling with doubt, the striving, the pursuit of your full potential. Isn't that what you were really after?

IT IS NOT THE CRITIC WHO COUNTS

Bill Belichick, head coach of the New England Patriots, has become as famous for his press conferences as he has for winning six Super Bowl Championships. To say he is a man of few words is a vast understatement. To say that he is not a media darling is fair. Some of us just don't have a bubbly, outgoing personality.

What is most interesting about his responses to reporters' questions isn't so much the number of words he uses but his tone and overall demeanor. You'd have to be utterly devoid of any emotional intelligence to not be able to see how thoroughly annoyed he gets with the whole idea of having to stand up behind a microphone and answer questions.

I don't think it's the mere fact that he must answer questions so much as it is the individuals asking the questions. The questions often can have a critical tone, and the reporters tend to imply that the coach should have or could have made better choices. The second-guessing of decisions is obviously extremely tough for Belichick to stomach. The reason seems obvious. I'm hypothesizing here, but there has to be a big part of his DNA that doesn't believe that he should have to be accountable to anyone who hasn't himself stepped inside the arena.

"It's not the critic who counts...."

For someone like Belichick, who has lived his entire adult life inside the arena, patience wears thin toward those whose job it is to criticize and *not* compete.

WHO KNOWS GREAT ENTHUSIASMS, THE GREAT DEVOTIONS...

Michael Jordan, considered by most people to be the greatest basketball player ever, was first a failure. During his sophomore year in high school, Jordan tried out for the basketball team but failed to make it. He was told he was too short to compete at the varsity level. For all his accomplishments, including six NBA championships, he failed way more than he succeeded.

He knew what the "great enthusiasms" felt like, but he also knew what it felt like to come up short "again and again." In Robert Goldman and Stephen Papson's book *Nike Culture: The Sign Of The Swoosh,* Jordan is quoted as having said, "I've missed over 9,000 shots in my career. I've lost almost 300 games. Twenty-six times I've been trusted to take the game-winning shot and missed. I've failed over and over and over again in my life. And that is why I succeed."

Jordan also embodied the "great devotions" necessary to exist and thrive inside the arena. During the 1997 NBA Finals against the Utah Jazz, Jordan and the Chicago Bulls found themselves tied in the series with the Jazz at two games apiece. The day before game 5, Jordan was diagnosed with food poisoning or the flu. If you've ever experienced the flu, you know that your biggest accomplishment during that time might be getting from the bed to the bathroom and back to the bed without incident.

But Jordan was anything but ordinary. He knew his team needed him to contribute something to the series' most pivotal game. The arena was where he belonged, flu or not. It's nearly impossible for competitors like Jordan to watch the game from a hotel bed. So he did the only thing he knew to do. He stepped inside regardless of whether he felt at his best or not.

There might not be another athlete on the planet that's had as big of an impact on his sport as Tiger Woods has had on golf. He is now past his prime and has suffered numerous setbacks, both professionally and personally. But he is considered by many to still be the biggest name in the sport and has inspired countless fans to grab their clubs and head to the course to try and emulate him.

Without question, he knows the "triumph of high achievement" as well as any athlete. In 1997, he became the youngest player to win the Masters Tournament at 21. As if the feeling of winning the sport's most famous event wasn't enough to put him on cloud nine, he walked off the final hole and collapsed into the arms of the person who'd made it his life's mission to make Tiger into a golf and cultural icon: his father Earl. Triumph personified.

Twenty-two years later, in 2019, he did it again after going eleven years without winning a major tournament and dealing with numerous injuries and personal problems. He won the Masters at the age of 43. This time, celebrating the win with his father, who had died thirteen years earlier, would be impossible. Instead, Tiger's son Charlie embraced his dad in the same spot where the father-son exchange occurred the first time.

These are the kinds of triumphs that movie writers look for when creating the next box-office blockbuster. But you can't make this stuff up. You could, but it wouldn't have the same effect. The audience, the fans, and anyone interested in the best of what makes us human can't help but be attracted to these stories because they actually happened. These weren't scenes rehearsed and acted out on a movie set. They played out live and in real-time. And it's just awesome to witness.

IN A WORTHY CAUSE

Then there are the times when athletes step into the arena with more on their minds than their personal sense of achievement. Sometimes, the individual players or entire teams realize that the meaning of the mission they are working on extends far beyond wins, losses, and statistics.

Take the Chicago Cubs, for example. The long-suffering Major League Baseball club from the Windy City won the World Series in 2016. The victory came 108 years after their last championship. During that century-plus stretch, the Cubs had become synonymous with the idea of losing. Every spring, the die-hard fans would suppress their hope for the coming season, believing the current season would just be a carbon copy of the one before.

With each season, it became more apparent that the "worthy cause" for the Cubs became winning a championship for the people of Chicago and less about the organization and its goals for itself. Bringing a sense of pride to the team's hard-working, loyal fans became much more important than hanging a banner at Wrigley Field. Generations of Cubs fans had attended games, cheered, spent money, and wore the apparel around the city through it all. The players that stepped into the arena day after day and year after year were doing it, not only for the promise of pride or satisfaction, but for those who weren't blessed with the opportunity or the desire to compete on the inside. It's incredible what can be accomplished when you're competing for something bigger than yourself.

All athletes were sports fans before they chose to test themselves on the inside. At first, they watched from a distance because watching can be wildly entertaining. That's why television networks purchase the rights (sometimes spending billions) to broadcast sports on their networks. There is such a high demand for sports entertainment. Millions want to watch. The fan wants to cheer for their team and imagine what it could feel like to hit the game-winning homer or raise the trophy above their heads.

But for some, watching isn't good enough. It doesn't satisfy the calling to roll up your sleeves and *do*. The only thing that could be better than watching these moments is living them.

What I love about the picture of the type of person that Roosevelt's speech paints is the same character trait that exemplifies the greatness of all the athletes mentioned above—courage. None of these athletes knew what the outcome would be ahead of time. There were never any guarantees. Jordan, Woods, the Chicago Cubs. They constantly faced resistance from people and forces that stood in their way, those who wanted them to fail. They also were bold enough to take the pressure and expectations of their biggest supporters onto their shoulders without being able to promise anyone that they would deliver.

The goal in sports is always to win, and winning is far and away the preferable outcome in every contest. But I would argue, as Roosevelt did, that once individuals have chosen to step inside the arena, they've already won.

All the athletes I've mentioned in this chapter are household names in the world of sports. Legends. World-class. And they all have something in common with each other. They possessed a fire deep inside themselves that transcended wins and losses—a fire so intense that it refused to be extinguished by sickness, injury, or mental or physical adversity. Regardless of any and all circumstances, they chose, courageously, to swallow hard and to step into the arena.

They chose to open themselves up to the critics.
They chose to never stand on the sidelines.
They chose to stick their hand in the fire.
And so did you.

A NEW ARENA

Eventually, the arena will be closed to every athlete. And then what? For a time, you were the man in the arena. You strived for greatness, stood firm against opponents, ignored the critics, and dug deep inside to master your skills and talents.

But now? You may feel like you're out of it. You've stepped out of the arena for the last time, feeling like you'll never again experience what it's like to step in, step up, and show out. But that is simply not the truth.

You're stepping now into a *new* arena. It's an arena with great possibilities and opportunities. Sure, it's one that's foreign, unknown, and far greater in size and magnitude. You might have to learn a few new rules and apply your skills in a slightly different way. But it will all be worth it because in this new arena, the greatest rewards await you

Stick Your Hand in the Fire

- What about your career makes you the most proud?
- What did you enjoy most about being an athlete?
- Did winning bring you joy or relief?
- Were you able to experience some level of satisfaction after a loss?

"The secret of change is to focus all of your energy not on fighting the old but building the new."

–Socrates

❷

WHEN THE FLAME FLICKERS

What's the one item you couldn't survive without? What's the first one that comes to mind? Maybe it's your phone or your favorite sweatshirt. Toothbrush? Chocolate-covered pretzels? How about your car?

One of the most popular reality TV shows on the Discovery Channel is *Naked and Afraid*. If you've never seen the show, its premise goes something like this: Two willing contestants, one male and one female, are dropped into a remote location somewhere in the world by plane, car, or boat. The chosen sites are not for the faint of heart. They are some of the harshest environments one could imagine, filled with all sorts of things to make a domesticated human extremely uncomfortable—from the swamps in the Louisiana Bayou to the Amazon rainforest and everything in between.

They then remove all their clothes and walk off into the woods to attempt to survive for twenty-one days. Because the two survivalists have never met each other before that day, the anxiety of a new relationship only adds to the situation's tension. If they don't "tap out" and quit before the 21-day period ends, they must embark on a long trek to their extraction point, where they are picked up and taken back to their previous reality.

They are permitted to carry a satchel over their shoulder that serves as a way to carry things such as materials for shelter or bugs that might become that night's dinner. (The satchel also provides a way to at least partially cover the parts of their body that would usually be covered.) They are also allowed to bring one survival item each. Possibilities include helpful tools, such as a knife or a machete. Some choose a mosquito net that can have many different uses.

If you were in their situation, would your answer to my question at the beginning of this chapter change? How so? Since the participants willingly signed up for this challenge, a cell phone wouldn't be needed to call for help. Luxury items and the things that make our existence more convenient would also be out the window. The most popular item chosen on the show by the contestants, the one they simply can't live without, is the fire starter. And if neither chooses the fire starter, the show gives it to them anyway.

Staring at the end of your athletic career can feel a lot like this scenario, at least at times. Your environment will look and feel different than it has in a long time. There may be fewer people that you interact with on a regular basis. The people that are around you may look like strangers. You may even ask yourself, "How did I get here?" In all likelihood, you will be removed from the surroundings that you've become accustomed to for so long, surroundings where you felt comfortable and safe. Suddenly, you are dropped into the middle of the unknown.

WHEN THE PLANE LANDS

The lights went out. They went out as quickly as you can flip a switch. The arena where you thrived and excelled is now closed. Not temporarily, but forever. The gates were padlocked, and your all-access pass was revoked. It was abrupt. And it was jarring.

Have you ever been asleep on an airplane when it landed? That's what the end of an athlete's career can feel like. The plane is moving so fast at such a smooth pace for so long that it can put you to sleep; it can feel like it's floating through the sky as if it doesn't have to think about where it's going or when it will arrive. It's almost as if it's on autopilot.

Then suddenly, the aircraft makes contact with the earth, and everything that's not bolted down or held in place by a seatbelt can shake and shift and rattle violently. Those who were under a cozy blanket and drooling on themselves are suddenly jolted back to consciousness.

When the wheels on my plane home from New York hit the ground, I wasn't asleep but felt the dread in my stomach intensify. Within about twelve hours, I had gone from suiting up for a pre-season game as a member of the New York Giants in front of 60,000 fans to returning to my hometown of Warren, Ohio. (You could fit the entire population of Warren into that stadium, with room to spare.) It hit me as my dad and I pulled out of the parking lot and headed for the house I grew up in.

I was headed back to where I had started. I had spent countless hours there dreaming of the scenario I had just experienced the day before. Posters of my heroes hung on my bedroom wall. The images of Dan Marino, Drew Bledsoe, and Brett Favre reminded me of what I was after. But now I realized that I had traveled in a large circle that landed me back where the trip had started five years earlier, with nothing to show for it. Or so it seemed.

There was no fanfare. There were no welcome home banners. There was no one to offer an encouraging word or a pat on the back. The phone wasn't ringing with a new opportunity on the other end of the line. Beyond my immediate family members, there were no recognizable faces. Nothing had changed in the town. Everything seemed so...normal.

But this wasn't my version of normal. It used to be, but not anymore. My reality for the several years before the end of my career consisted of press conferences, plane rides to new locations, and a fast-paced existence.

It now felt as if I had left this world five years earlier and set off on a voyage around the world. One that was full of exciting adventures and unexpected surprises. One filled with challenges to be faced and treasures to be discovered. Then, it was all over just like that, and I was back to the beginning.

This now seemed like an alternate universe. It was one that I didn't feel like I belonged in, even though it was the one that had shaped me years before. It was odd to realize that the environment hadn't changed much. So why did it seem so different? So small?

I now had plenty of time to search for those answers.

Take a deep breath

When your real or proverbial plane lands, hit the pause button for a minute. It may be uncomfortable to attempt to focus on nothing, allowing yourself simply to be where you are at the moment. But your body and mind are so used to pushing forward to what is next. It's okay— maybe even necessary—to take a deep breath. You've absorbed and given great energy throughout your time in your sport. Allowing yourself the grace to acknowledge that time and reflect is extremely important if you are going to reach even higher in the future. Sometimes you have to take a step back to move forward.

Allow yourself the freedom to stop moving. Not forever, but for however long it takes to realize how fast you were going. This may be the first time in years that you haven't had to operate on all cylinders. That may be difficult to see at first, and that realization may take some time. It can be revealing to realize the presence of things only after they are gone. For example, you may find yourself sleeping a little heavier after your career ends. Why would that be the case? Could it be from the absence of anticipation about the next morning's practice session?

Examine these types of changes as you notice them. Sometimes these signals will feel like a relief, and others will cause a quick bout of anxiety. The task here is to practice becoming aware of what you need now. Computers need to be shut down and rebooted after working extremely hard for long stretches of time. High-performing athletes are no different.

You don't have to have it all figured out today

Your mental programming as an athlete will have you asking yourself what can be done to improve your situation. You'll wonder what you could or should be working on to move things along. While this may feel like the right thing to do, resist the temptation to figure everything out quickly. When you accidentally drift slightly outside the lines while driving on the highway, the urge is to jerk the wheel to promptly get back in your lane. This can cause tension, and this abrupt course correction can sometimes cause accidents. You will get there gradually and with patience.

It is common for athletes to always know exactly what to do next. Practice schedules, games, and other activities are usually planned out weeks in advance. How many times did you show up for practice only to find there were no drills planned for you that day? Probably not many. Time was of the essence, and efficiency was critical. Even when you were on your own, you had been given instructions on what to do, what to eat, to get enough rest, and what to be thinking about for the next in-person session. There wasn't a great deal for you to figure out. All you had to do was show up.

Now, without everything laid out for you, you have some weighty but rewarding work ahead. To rush into the unknown in a panic without the proper knowledge and skill set would be foolish and potentially dangerous. Even the contestants on *Naked and Afraid* realize that they have to pace themselves to make clearheaded decisions about basics like where to set up their camp and what material to use to construct their shelter.

This is a pivotal time in your life. Give yourself the necessary time to hear the questions you will be asked and let the answers develop.

As we will discuss in future chapters, this journey belongs to you and no one else. You may encounter friends and family who will apply pressure on you (even if unintentional) to figure things out quickly. Don't give in to it.

Along with external influences, there may be an additional internal voice that shows up: Guilt. When you've been so active in applying yourself and reaching to improve daily, and then one day you're not, you can start feeling guilty. Gone are the days of putting in long hours because you were committed to a cause. Don't beat yourself up if you have a few extra hours on your hands. You likely wished you had more free time when you were an athlete. Now that you have it, you may feel like you should be doing something.

WHAT'S MISSING?

10 things that you didn't know you needed

One of my favorite memories from my childhood was our family's annual trip to Kennywood Amusement Park located just outside of Pittsburgh. Next to Christmas, this was the best day of the year. We'd arrive when it opened and stay until it was pitch black so we could ride the roller coasters up into the dark sky. I would be in tears when my parents said it was time to leave. But as I headed toward my late teens, I started to take an interest in other things and was preparing for the big transition to college. So the trips to the park became few and far between.

After completing my freshman year in college, my best friend Tom Moore and I decided to head back to the park and have some fun since we attended different universities in different states and hadn't seen each other much over the last year. At the end of the day, we started to walk to the exit. After a few steps, Tom stopped walking and quickly patted the pockets of his jeans. He had lost his car keys.

Inside a huge amusement park, those keys could be anywhere. Where do you start looking? Finding those keys sounded like an impossible task. We felt defeated before we even began looking. They could've been at the bottom of a ravine hundreds of feet below the coaster tracks. Without much hope, we first headed for the lost and found. Did the park even have a lost and found? And if so, would anyone take the time to pick them up and return them? If not, how would I get home?

Amazingly, the keys were there. I actually couldn't believe it.

At this point, as you transition from one arena to another, it's easy to feel like you've lost everything important to you. As hard as it may be to believe at the time, you can get back the essential elements needed to re-ignite your fire.

But first, you need to have the knowledge of what those things are. Just like with Tom's keys at Kennywood, we had to acknowledge what was lost. And in time, and with the help of a supporter or two who wants to help you get back on track, you'll be on your way. But

37

it all starts with *knowledge*, your own personal lost and found box. Check it first when you find yourself needing answers.

Truth is, all these things may be missing...but not gone forever.

Financial support and security

There is no need more urgent than the need to be able to support yourself financially when your career comes to an end. Financial struggles will lead to a feeling of being exposed. While it's necessary to find a way to earn money to take care of yourself and your basic needs, don't make the mistake of thinking that money will fill the void that's been left by the absence of your sport.

In many cases, because of family support or scholarships, finances and the basic needs that they cover were addressed one way or another. Although everyone was always trying to figure out how to have more of it, money wasn't a top priority. Now, you might just realize that earning money has moved up quite a few rungs on the priority ladder. When your athletic career ends, it becomes apparent that the free (or mostly free) ride ends too.

When the money question is addressed, at least temporarily, you are free to focus on the bigger questions. The deeper and more important questions. How many friends or former teammates do you know right now whose only concern is money? What if instead of devoting that time and effort to acquiring money, they directed it towards educating themselves on how money really works and how to make it work for them? Don't chase money. Figure out how to make it come to you.

Money and financial support can be an enormous distraction. They can and at some point will weigh on your mind, adding pressure to an already difficult transition period. But keep your eyes on the prize. What's the ultimate prize? We are going to talk about that in the next chapter, but I'll give you a hint: it's *not* money.

Too narrow of a focus on money and what it will provide you will inevitably lead to missed opportunities. Saying no to those opportunities because of a lack of funds or a need to make more will have you looking back with regret years later. When opportunities come into your life, you want to be able to evaluate those open doors with a clear head, especially when those possibilities excite you. Don't let the need for money blindfold you when you may already feel like you are searching for what's missing in the dark.

Clarity

One of the biggest and most important things athletes struggle with in life after sports is the loss of a clear idea of what to do and who you are while doing it. Why is having clarity important and what does it do for you? How did sports provide that for you? Having a sense of belonging and a place in the world helps you prioritize your life.

During your career, you made plans and organized your schedule, or had it done for you. And you no doubt focused on short- and long-term goals. Your sense of clarity gave your life definition and provided a great deal of pleasure and satisfaction. It provided you an avenue to increase the level of your health and created friendships that last a lifetime.

Many people are born knowing exactly what they want to do. Many of us athletes fall into this category, but the problem is that we can't play competitively forever. The good news is your purpose can change, evolve, and grow. We just have to put in the work to uncover what it is that matters to you the way athletics mattered.

Structure

Athletes love structure. If every one of the ten missing elements in this section received an award at the end-of-the-year team banquet, structure would win the "Unsung Hero" award. Without it, you would've accomplished a lot less during your career and those accomplishments would've taken much longer to achieve or wouldn't have happened at all. Now it's going to be up to you to install and enforce that same structure in your life.

Think about how integral a routine was to your success. Structure defined what you did and what you didn't do. It established clear guardrails around your days to prevent anything that wasn't in line with your goals from knocking you off your chosen path. The boring and often underappreciated asset called structure provided you with limits, set sturdy boundaries around you, and set clear expectations for yourself.

Rhythm and consistency are made possible with structure, not only in your days but in your life as a whole. When you don't have to think, you can move more quickly and easily toward improvement. Not having to spend energy on making decisions about where you're going to be at a certain time and what you'll be doing will lead to gradual and smooth progression in the right direction. This leads to big advancements over time.

Without proper planning of your days, the tendency is to drift. Like floating on a raft in the middle of a lake on a windy day, you'll have little to no control over where you're headed without structure powering your movement.

You can grab your own free copy of my structure checklist here: **outsidethearena.com/structure**

Fun

Let's face it. More than likely, the reason athletes begin playing sports in the first place as kids is because it was fun. It's fun to feel the rush of exerting yourself in pursuit of a win. And we all know how we feel when we win. It makes us want to play again and again.

It also feels good to challenge yourself physically and to feel fulfilled from giving the competition your all. Even the sportsmanship and respect that you feel for your competitors is sometimes unstated but appreciated.

Challenge

Athletes love the thrill of competition. They have no problem risking the agony of losing in exchange for the chance to test themselves to see if they can come out of the battle on top and as the winner. While winning can be extremely gratifying, the real satisfaction comes from testing yourself against who you were yesterday and the limits of what you're capable of tomorrow.

The late nights, the long practices, the extra work when friends are having fun, the sacrifices. What would motivate someone to choose these things over the thousands of temptations begging us to give in? People with an internal fire and drive enjoy doing these hard things because it feels good knowing that you can stand out by being willing to do the hard thing, which also builds resilience for the next time you are faced with something difficult.

Confidence

The challenges that you've faced and the dedication that you've shown have given you a tremendous gift: confidence. Knowing that you've been through difficult times and pushed through can build a level of self-confidence that most people aren't equipped with. But the confidence that you feel inside your athletic comfort zone comes mainly from the fact that you've put in the reps. The repetitive work on your forehand, the endless free throws after everyone has left the gym, or hitting an extra bucket of balls at the driving range all can give you the self-assurance, faith, and trust that you're prepared for greatness the next time the lights are on and the game is on the line.

Pride

Where does pride come from and what does it feel like? Not the pride that can easily spill into arrogance, but the emotion that we feel when we achieve something great. Of course, we can also feel pride for someone else. What was the last thing you accomplished, big or small? How did it feel when you accomplished it? When pride is strong, often it's difficult to not express it outwardly in some fashion. There's a bounce in your step and you hold your head up a little higher, or you can't help but smile or walk a little taller. There's no better avenue than sports to allow you the opportunity to feel proud of yourself.

Recognition

The applause, the pats on the back, the repeated messages of "great game", or "good job." Whether we realized it or not, we became accustomed to hearing the encouragement and positive feedback during the time we played. We became addicted to it. How could we not? It felt good! Medals, trophies, and awards all became visual reminders of what we were accomplishing.

Athletes are admired for their unique talents. During your career, you may have heard from family members or people who you haven't spoken with in years because they are interested in what you are achieving in your sport. You may have even received messages from complete strangers congratulating you on a win. What might have begun as a fun game that you simply enjoyed playing turns into a way to fulfill one of your most important needs as a human being. Being an athlete might be one of the best ways to know that you are seen, heard, and valued.

Comradery

Ask any former athlete who played a team sport what they miss most about their playing days and you'll probably hear very few mentions of the games, the wins, the applause, or the awards. The answer you are most likely to hear is "I miss my teammates." Gone are the jokes in the locker room, the shared love of the game, and the challenge of competing against one another in practice or in the weight room. You might most remember the difficult times, like running the stadium steps in the July heat, sweating through practices, or rehabbing an injury in the team training room. You definitely remember that you did these difficult things not by yourself, but with your teammates.

You knew exactly what your out-of-breath teammate's lungs felt like and what doubts were creeping into his or her mind as they struggled to finish the last sprint after a hard practice. Not because you were an observer who felt bad for them but because you were an active participant who knew the pain they were experiencing. Empathy was not a word I used or heard mentioned in any locker room during my career, but I felt it every day.

Impact

Whether you realize it or not, because of your ability, talent, and hard work, you made an impact on people. The individuals you affected reached beyond just your family and friends. You may not have ever met the individuals whose lives you affected, but they are out there in the world, and they remember what you accomplished. Maybe you hit a winning forehand during a tennis match that impressed a fan or maybe you hung your hat on out-hustling everyone else on the soccer field and that made an onlooker see a little of herself in you. Maybe an observer of your career really liked your character and the way you handled yourself during the tough times.

It's almost impossible to know what type of an impact you had on everyone because you simply can't meet everyone that has watched you perform. But make no mistake about it, you left an impression. And maybe even inspired someone to work a little harder or aspire to be just like you.

Being plucked out of a comfortable and familiar bubble of the arena then dropped into what looks and feels like an entirely different world can feel daunting and disorienting. New obstacles will emerge, much will *feel* like it's missing, and the people in your world may be complete strangers. And with these new circumstances come new challenges that need to be met in order to one day triumph again.

Starting small, taking one step at a time, and finding small wins will leave you feeling less vulnerable and more capable of processing the details of what's happening to you. Slowly but surely you will find answers, fill in gaps, and move forward.

Has your cage been rattled? Yes. But remember this truth: you already have what you need. The skills and experience you acquired as an athlete provide you with the foundation to reach even higher, and your resilience gives you the will to keep going.

But deep within you lives something even more important than those things: *the fire to be great again.* Do you still have it? Do you still feel it? Of course you do. Where exactly does that fire come from? It's the final piece of the knowledge puzzle.

Stick Your Hand in the Fire

- What did your world look like when your "plane landed"?
- What was the most shocking or unexpected thing that you experienced in the immediate aftermath?
- What is the #1 thing you're struggling with now?
- What aspect of being an athlete do you miss the most?

"When a person can't find a deep sense of meaning, they distract themselves with pleasure."

–Victor Frankl

❸
THROUGH THE SMOKE

I'm an avid listener of podcasts. I devour them whenever I can. Driving in the car, working out in the gym, even in the shower. I'm always looking for new and interesting stories and people that I can be inspired by and learn from. I recently discovered *The School of Greatness Podcast* hosted by Lewis Howes, and one particular episode caught my attention. It was an interview with a former football player named Inky Johnson. More interesting than his name was his story.

Inky Johnson was on his way to living his dream of playing in the NFL. By his junior year as a University of Tennessee cornerback, he was already attracting the attention of scouts who were projecting him as a top pick. But on a gameday in September of 2006, those dreams came to an end. On a routine tackle, Johnson sustained a career-ending (and at the time, life-threatening) injury that resulted in permanent paralysis of his right arm and hand.

Inky found meaning after his injury by dedicating his life to inspiring and motivating others. He became a dynamic motivational speaker and began sharing his story to help others realize their full potential and inspire them to overcome challenges. Through his speeches, he emphasizes the importance of mindset, perseverance, and faith in achieving greatness. In addition, he also started the Inky

Johnson Foundation, where he mentors young people and helps them develop the tools and mindset necessary to succeed in life.

The end of Inky's career came abruptly before his eligibility expired on its own. Initially, he intended to play the game he loved again one day. But it wasn't meant to be. What was meant to be was revealed to him after some resistance. He had to (like you will too) let go of the thing that he thought defined who he was and what he was meant to do. The pleasure and happiness that he derived from playing football would eventually pale in comparison to the bigger purpose he found, one he never anticipated during his playing days.

THE PLEASURE PRINCIPLE

Pleasure. Isn't that what we are all chasing? Some call it happiness, but chasing happiness might just be a game that can't be won. Don't get me wrong, I'm not in any way saying that you're doomed to live an unhappy life. But you'll need to make an important distinction between pleasure (or happiness) and *meaning*.

Sigmund Freud, an Austrian neurologist, is widely considered to be "the father of modern psychology." He created the concept of psychoanalysis and has influenced many of the theories that we in the Western world adhere to today. His work encompassed theories that spanned the topics of sex, the parent-child relationship, and even dreams. He coined terms and phrases that still are commonly used in daily life.

Freud formulated *the pleasure principle* after studying the behavior of children. He observed that because we all have basic needs like water, food, shelter, and various other desires that we want fulfilled, children didn't put a great deal of thought into whether or not their urges were providing *meaning*. They just sought to satisfy their urges. It's natural to want more of a good thing. Interestingly, Freud also noticed that kids tend to act on their impulses rapidly to achieve pleasure.

Children usually get a free pass when it comes to acting without thinking. We understand that they are still learning and developing. As an adult, though, we've already used up all our free passes to quench our immediate thirst. Try cutting the line at your favorite Starbucks because you want your caffeine and you want it now. See how that goes over. (I've had the urge to sometimes do exactly that. Okay, *all* the time.)

But if I had jumped the line and satisfied my most immediate need, I doubt that I would've felt much meaning. I'm actually positive that I would've felt worse than I did before sipping my morning pick-me-up. Not only would that not have been a meaningful incident, but I would have experienced a meaning *deficiency*. Let's not forget that meaning can be found through a deed or a task, through relationships, or through suffering. The Starbucks scenario satisfies none of those.

So what meaning can I find in being the sixteenth person in the Starbucks line when there is only one barista working behind the counter and I'm running a little late to an appointment? Acknowledging the opportunity to practice patience by listening to another ten minutes of a podcast episode would have provided some meaning. Better yet, making someone's day by allowing them to move into the spot before me in line would have done the trick too. Paying for a stranger's latte would definitely have created a meaningful moment not only for me but for them as well.

So, are you pursuing happiness or meaning?

Happiness is a side effect

I'm willing to bet that you've spent your fair share of time on the treadmill during your athletic career. Maybe you're spending more time on it now that you're retired. But have you ever been on a hedonic treadmill?

You might not have heard of it before, but I'm sure you've experienced it. We all have at one point or another. It's not an actual treadmill used to improve your physical fitness. It's an idea in the psychology world that can help explain why you may feel a letdown after acquiring something that you thought would make you happy.

It goes like this. You, me, and everyone else have a set baseline happiness point: how you are before anything exciting happens. It's your "vibe", how you carry yourself from a general happiness perspective. Are you always up, a little low, or somewhere in between? It exists before you buy your dream car or drink your favorite beverage from the Stanley Cup after finishing the season as NHL Champs.

Do you know where I'm going with this? What have you purchased recently that you were really excited about? Did you feel as excited, say a month after the purchase as you did on day two? Did the shiny object change the core of who you are even though it might have made you feel differently right after you bought it? I doubt it. Once the novelty wears off, you return to your prior level of happiness, and you start searching for the next thing to bring you up again.

The misconception is that our happiness is fueled only by external factors and circumstances. Researchers discovered during a study in 1971 that lottery winners returned to their level of happiness after winning large sums of money, and paraplegics also returned to the same level of happiness before the accident. So lottery winners were no happier than the paraplegics whose bodies were paralyzed. Both groups returned to their original levels whether that meant going down from the high of winning an unfathomable amount of money or rising up from an initially devastating setback. What can we all learn from this? Happiness is temporary and constantly changing where we think it can be found.

Too few of us have our eyes on the right things and aren't looking for meaning in the right places. Too often, we get caught up in the short-sighted need to be "happy." Shouldn't there be something else to the equation? You can feel it when there isn't. You can sense when meaning is missing. Continuing to stay on the hedonic treadmill is like running on an actual treadmill only to focus on the number of calories burned instead of the goal of living a long healthy life.

"It can't be pursued, it must ensue."

"When I have X, then I'll be happy." We've all played this game with ourselves. And I think we know on some level that it simply isn't true. But we continue to try to fool ourselves into believing that it is. Why do we do that? If I have X amount of money, *then* I'll be happy. If I lose ten pounds, *then* I will feel content. If I lead the league in assists, then I'll win MVP and *that* will make me happy.

Instead of pursuing happiness, you must *allow* it to happen. But how? By not caring about it, according to Victor Frankl, author of *Man's Search for Meaning*.

This will be difficult to wrap your brain around at first, and I speak from experience on that one. Take a moment to reflect on the reasons that being an athlete made you happy. What were the causes? If you tap into those, I think you may discover that at the top of the list sits a cause or reason greater than yourself. What do you think? I know that you played, at least in part, for you. But is that where the true meaning was?

IDENTITY CRISIS

What defines you? And if you know the answer, are you comfortable with it? Having a blueprint, playbook, or any type of plan for your life is important. That much you already should know. You can't figure out *how* to get to where you want to go without knowing *where* you want to go first. But there is something much more important. It's a step that so many athletes never stop to contemplate.

Who are you? Right now. Take away what you do for a living, the fact that you were an athlete, who your family is, or where you're from. What type of person are you? How did you become that person? How did you end up standing in the exact spot you are standing in now? These are not easy questions to answer. Most of us don't know the answers and too often, don't want to know the answers out of fear of not liking what we discover. But before you begin to tap into your true potential, you must first know who you are dealing with.

How do you see yourself?

For you, the job of figuring out who you were probably was an easy one. It's likely not something you had to think much about. From an early age, your talents were recognized by parents and others who noticed the physical skills that set you apart from other kids. Sports was "your thing."

But now, has sports become your "only" thing? This is the case for so many players. You see yourself as an athlete, but is that all you see when you look at the person staring back at you in the mirror? One dimension?

If that is where your mindset is right now, hear this loud and clear: *You are not just one thing.* Long before you became an athlete you were something much more important—a human being. Someone completely unique. You are the result of your upbringing, your DNA, your environment, what words you heard, what part of the country you lived in, and millions of other things. A huge percentage of these will remain with you for the rest of your life.

How do others see you?

In the classic 1985 coming-of-age movie, *The Breakfast Club*, five high school students from five different cliques serve their detention for nine hours on a Saturday in the school library. Principal Vernon, who would also love to be anywhere else but at school on a Saturday, fails miserably at trying to control the group. Determined to teach them a lesson, he gives them an assignment that they must complete by the end of the day. The students are to write an essay describing who they think they are. One of the students, Brian Johnson, ("the Brain") begins to play with his pen as he ponders the question "Who are you?"

After spending the majority of the day getting to know each other, breaking out of the library, returning without being caught, vandalizing the space, and revealing to each other why they received the detention in the first place, the students realize that the essays still haven't been completed.

Tasked with writing everyone's essay, Brian cleverly and sarcastically writes that they all think Principal Vernon is crazy to ask them to write an essay about who they think they are. His reason? Because Vernon (along with the rest of the world) sees each of them how they want to see them—as a brainiac, a princess, a jock, a criminal, and a basket case. And while this is also how they might have started the day viewing themselves and each other, by the end of the film, a transformation had occurred.

Their identity was no longer built from what others saw in them, or even from a narrow view they may have had of themselves. They realized that they were complex human beings that didn't fit a single definition.

THE QUEST FOR MEANING

Man's Search For Meaning is probably one of the most impactful books of our time. Author Victor Frankl details his account of being held captive in a German concentration camp during World War II. Frankl and his fellow prisoners were not held captive with the notion that their imprisonment would only be temporary. They were there to be exterminated by the Nazis. Frankl, an Austrian neurologist and psychologist, closely observed the prisoners and studied the differences between those who survived and those who did not. The result of his findings led him to create his philosophy: logotherapy.

While in the camps, he noticed that there was quite a distinction between the thoughts and actions of his fellow captives. Some resigned themselves to the fact that they were going to die. Others seemed to hang on to hope and maintain a focus on something in the future. A goal or something they wanted to accomplish at some future point in time. In the most unimaginably dire circumstances, they found a spirit to think with their mind centered on what lies ahead. Even in the face of groups of prisoners being selected to enter the gas chambers to take their last breath, others found reasons to endure.

Man's Search for Meaning

I believe inside of all of us is a drive. A pull towards something. Have you felt it in you? I have to admit, though, that I feel like I have done more pushing than pulling. I spent way too much time looking back to the past for a response to those nagging feelings, wanting to make sense of my career and what it meant to me then and what it is supposed to mean now. Does it carry any weight today even though it ended two decades ago?

The following is an excerpt from *Man's Search for Meaning* that shows how some of the concentration camp's prisoners chose to see their surroundings. It can also shed some light on how athletes like us can begin to view the end of the most meaningful period in our lives with a certain perspective.

> "A man who let himself decline because he could not see any future goal found himself occupied with retrospective thoughts. In a different connection, we have already spoken of the tendency there was to look into the past, to help make the present, with all its horrors, less real. But in robbing the present of its reality there lay a certain danger. It became easy to overlook the opportunities to make something positive of camp life, opportunities which really did exist...Such people forgot that often it is just such an exceptionally difficult external situation which gives man the opportunity to grow spiritually beyond himself. Instead of taking the camp's difficulties as a test of their inner strength, they did not take their life seriously and despised it as something of no consequence. They preferred to close their eyes and to live in the past. Life for such people became meaningless."

Some of the prisoners found meaning in things like shaving their faces with glass, wearing the same clothes every day until they started to disintegrate, and being beaten to within an inch of death. A few even saw the meaning in death itself.

If some of the inmates in the concentration camps could find value and meaning in the middle of extreme circumstances, you can certainly find meaning in your life.

Meaning is the motivation

Your search for meaning in your life should be your primary motivation. Not pleasure in all its forms, and certainly not power. It helps me to pay attention to the words that I choose when thinking about meaning and my quest for it in my life. I choose to focus on the meaning "in my life" as opposed to the meaning "of my life." These ideas have provided me and my view of my lifelong love affair with sports with a new and hopeful perspective.

What motivates you? The answer to that question will be different for everyone. For all of us, the answers are tied to something in the future. We can't use motivation to accomplish anything in the past. And our actions in the present are, of course, tied to our future. When we understand that meaning is what we are after and we begin to look for it, we'll have all the motivation we could ever need.

I think it's important to note that the majority of the prisoners were not able to get past the hopelessness, the grief, the loss of individual freedoms, and the loss of basic human rights. But a few did achieve a level of greatness. It's fascinating to me to think about whether they would have achieved this greatness or this great perspective without being thrust into that devastating environment. Most athletes, like the largest group of prisoners, tend to believe that the great moments in their lives have already happened in the past. *Are my best days over?* Do you feel that way about your life and your time in the arena?

Frankl believed meaning in your life could be found in three different places. The first is in **work** or the pursuit of some significant endeavor. (My own struggles with life on the outside can be traced to my giving too much attention to only this one category.) The second is love or **relationships**. And finally, meaning can be found in **suffering**.

Work (Significance)

The mistake that too many athletes make is attaching the meaning of their lives as a whole to their work and their work alone. We see and hear about this every day. The business owner who dies shortly after his or her retirement because, in their mind, the work ended so meaning ceased to exist as well. Or the coach who dies shortly after their decades-long career comes to an end.

For me, football was the sole meaning in my life. As it turns out, this was a mistake. But I felt this way because I didn't have the knowledge of how all of my eggs were in that one basket. The higher you ascend through the athletic ranks, the more it will appear as if that part of your life is the central meaning of it. Set your mind's camera to take a much wider snapshot of where your past career and your future work fit into the overall significance of your life and the resulting happiness that you will experience.

Relationships (Love)

As human beings, we all have relationships in our lives. Some of them are good and a few might be toxic. Some take effort to maintain, and some seem to come without any bumps in the road. You can find meaning in all of them.

I have two children. As I write this, my son Blake is 14 and my daughter Brooklyn is 12. Both have given unspeakable amounts of meaning to my life. Blake is athletic and has a tremendous ability to remember important dates and events, especially those related to sports. He makes me laugh until my stomach hurts with his spot-on impersonations of sports broadcasters like Jim Nantz, Sean McDonough, and Gus Johnson. Brooklyn is kind and is quick to lend a hand without being asked. Her energy lights up every room that she walks into. Or cartwheels into. These are just a couple of the countless reasons that my wife Christina and I love our kids.

But why do so many of us have children? Sure, maybe to carry on the family name or pass on the family legacy. These are worthwhile reasons. But Frankl has painted a much deeper and clearer picture for me. He wrote about what it really means to love another person and how to truly find meaning in that relationship. This is what's possible when you love someone else, and nothing could ring truer when I think about Blake and Brooklyn.

To love them is to know their essential traits.

Because of the love we have for them, we can see the potential that they possess.

Through this love, we help them to see their potential.

Through this new knowledge, their potential can be fulfilled.

Isn't this why we have children? If you don't have kids, think about the person you love most in the world. Do the above steps hold true for you?

As an athlete, you were in a unique position to develop extremely deep and meaningful relationships with your teammates. Think about it. Was there one teammate whom you mentored or took under your wing? Why was that? Why them?

You may be hurting now because you're feeling unsure of who you are. And you're grieving the loss of something very important to you. But here is a surefire path to meaning: find somebody to love.

Suffering

The third and final path to meaning is to examine the suffering in your life. It exists for a reason. It has great significance, if you can be open to just how it can be turned on its head and be used to your advantage.

I should mention that Frankl writes that suffering isn't necessary to find meaning but when unavoidable, meaning can be found as a result. If you are like me, there has already been a certain amount of suffering over the end of your playing days. It might be tough to admit because suffering sounds so extreme. And again, athletes are trained to never reveal chinks in their armor.

Suffering can manifest itself in different ways, though. For most, the suffering is quiet, as if to not raise any red flags. You don't want to set off any alarm bells that may signal a weakness in your warrior exterior. If the word suffering sounds too much like playing defense, go ahead and switch it to "courage under fire." Whatever phrase you use, you will encounter it.

The suffering you have experienced, are experiencing, or will experience in the future can have meaning. While in the concentration camp, Frankl at one point had to turn in his clothes and exchange them for ones that were no longer needed by an inmate who had been murdered.

Tucked within the inside pocket of Frankl's jacket was the manuscript for his book. It was all he had worked for and was determined to somehow get those words to the rest of the world in hopes that they would help someone. But when he was forced to turn in those clothes, the pages were lost. It later occurred to him that having lost the manuscript was a calling to live out his thoughts instead of just writing them down on paper.

"Suffering ceases to be suffering at the moment it finds a meaning," Frankl wrote. The pain, stress, or quiet frustration you feel can be taken away if you can do the work of attaching a meaning to it. You bravely suffered for your sport. You suffered while inside the arena. The suffering was part of the deal. It played a pivotal role in your career whether you realized it or not. You grew to be comfortable with it, maybe even enjoyed it or took pride in it. You looked at the suffering as a challenge to be overcome. You found meaning in it. You can do it again. You can do it now.

Stick Your Hand in the Fire

- Are you chasing happiness or meaningful moments?
- Do you see yourself as anything other than an athlete? If so, what or who?
- What will be your motivation moving forward?
- What does your career mean now that it's over?

Train your brain to look for meaning in the mundane and watch what happens.

I

Part Two

INSPIRED INTENTION

Mark Cuban knew what he wanted. He wanted more. More than he grew up with. He was raised in a middle-class family in the suburbs of Pittsburgh, Pennsylvania, and saw his grandfather, a Russian immigrant, hustle to take care of his family. Morris Chobanisky (who would later change the family name to Cuban) showed young Mark the value of perseverance by selling various items out of the trunk of his car. Mark modeled the go-getter habits of his grandfather by selling garbage bags door to door just to earn extra money for an expensive pair of shoes that he had his eye on. He also sold stamps and newspapers.

By the time he reached high school, he had set an intention to become an entrepreneur. He offered dance lessons and opened a bar to put himself through college at the University of Indiana. Despite the pull of being his own boss, Cuban took various jobs working for companies like Mellon Bank after graduating from college.

After being fired from his position as a salesperson for a software company, Cuban finally had enough and set out to do things his way by opening his own company. He didn't know exactly what the details would be or whether he would be successful, but he knew what he intended to do.

Not only has Cuban become a successful entrepreneur, but he is the billionaire owner of the Dallas Mavericks. Given all his professional success, it would've been easy for Cuban to rest on his accomplishments. But Cuban set a new intention to inspire the next generation of entrepreneurs. He is now the star of the wildly popular show Shark Tank, where he has spent years investing in people with dreams like the ones he had and inspiring them to never let those dreams die.

Now you have some fierce knowledge and have begun to understand what attracted you to the athletic arena, what it gave you that's now missing, and why your crusade for meaning is so important. Now it's time to be *intentional*. That starts with understanding who you are now as an individual, a person, and a human. More importantly, it requires making choices about who you want to be, tomorrow and in the coming years.

I feel most alive when I feel inspired. I believe that's why sports are so popular throughout the world. It's certainly what has kept me coming back to watch as a fan after my time as a player ended.

Doesn't sports offer observers and fans a personal benefit, something for them that goes beyond just entertainment value? Fans are inspired by the athletes who throw themselves into the arena and dare greatly. It's less about what the athletes are accomplishing and more about how their actions inspire the onlookers to use the inspiration they are feeling to be intentional in their own lives. Greatness is what we all aspire to reach in our own lives. Some let the inspiration fade, and some take the next step. The key is to connect the emotion to the intention.

In the previous chapters, I've asked you some questions to help you reflect and become more self-aware. Hopefully, you've asked yourself questions too. Now, it's time to make some statements that will stir up some emotion.

Where questions can take time to work through, intentions can give you a quick hit of adrenaline and a jolt of inspiration. They can pull you instead of pushing you. Simply stating what you intend to do or who you intend to be can strengthen you. Intentions are powerful even if you don't yet know how you'll accomplish them. You have the power to create a new reality for yourself. And although intentions are an important step in building meaning into your present and your future, they aren't the complete picture. You'll build the new version of you one layer at a time, one dream at a time, one decision at a time, and one discipline at a time.

"The soul becomes dyed with the color of its thoughts."

—Marcus Aurelius

❹
MENTAL DYNAMITE

Get your mind right.

Inside the arena, there is a certain mindset that is required for excellence. Toughness, attention to detail, persistence, and focus are just a few of the traits needed to be great at what you do on the field or on the court. A strong mind can be what separates the good players from the champions in the most clutch moments. But when the fans watch warriors compete on the inside, it's what they *can't* see that is often the difference between triumph and defeat. Not the unbelievable sideline catch or the three-pointer from the logo.

The greatest battle you will fight now that your career has ended is overcoming the obstacles that exist in your own mind. How do you, the person, think? Not the athlete, but you the human.

Before you became an athlete, and certainly before you peaked as an athlete, you possessed patterns. Ways of thinking that were the result of many different factors. The thoughts, beliefs, and behaviors about yourself and the outside world make up who you currently are, and they will impact how you react to what happens to you and the results you achieve.

These patterns of thinking were shaped by your immediate family, friends, and the environment you grew up in. They may have laid dormant because they weren't relevant to the immediate challenges that you faced. Or, the more likely scenario, they were masked by the encouragement of coaches and teammates. The positivity of your athletic environment probably prohibited you from falling into bad thought patterns.

Now that you'll be stepping into a new arena, you will have to be vigilant for the patterns that you carry with you every day. Because of the drive and ambition that you acquired as an athlete, you might believe that you will be able to muscle your way to meaning, believing that you can rely solely on skills and action to provide a meaningful life is a mistake.

The good news is your mind can be developed, altered, and shaped to make you virtually unstoppable.

The first step to becoming more self-aware is to know what to be more aware of. Your job is not to judge. It is to listen to the voice inside yourself, ask it questions, and record the data. Yes, this could lead to catching the side-eye from strangers in the grocery store. So what! Throughout this process, I've learned that I shouldn't care so much about what others might think of me.

Let's look at how to assess parts of your mental toughness that will allow you to know what needs improvement as you prepare for life on the outside.

THE WAR INSIDE

At this stage, it's extremely important to tell yourself the truth. You think you know yourself well, but if you dig deeper, sometimes you can be surprised by what you can discover. When you have a good grasp on yourself, you know what your strengths are, and you also can be honest with yourself about your weaknesses. You become more comfortable with who you are even if there are still things that you'd like to change. Finally, you begin to fear failure less and less.

Undertaking this process forces you to reflect and pay attention. And when you can begin to rely less on emotions, you tend to make better decisions. If you can begin to analyze not only yourself but the others around you as well, you can begin to build empathy. Attempting to understand the other person's point of view can be one of the most important ways to build strong relationships.

Being in tune with your emotions also helps you to see how to best assess a situation and decide on the best way to respond. Life isn't about what happens to you, it's all about how you react to what happens to you. And those reactions can have a huge impact on your success. When you practice being aware, you usually start to give some additional attention to things beyond yourself. For example, developing an active listening habit can lead to better conversations and better boundaries with the people in your life.

When you zoom out on a situation or problem, you tend to consider many things that might have led to or produced a result. The more angles you consider, the better equipped you are to move forward with a better understanding of the situation. When you know what your starting point is, you can begin to change. When you know what your strengths and weaknesses are, you can go to work on them and start making progress towards a better tomorrow. The goal of becoming more aware is not to criticize, find fault with, or judge yourself. It is simply to learn where you are now so you can more clearly define where you want to go and who you want to be in the future.

Player vs. Victim

One of these internal battles we can have is whether we are acting as a player or victim, which comes down to a focus on either what you can control or what you can't. Victims focus their attention on things that they cannot influence, like outside forces and other people. Blame is a big part of their game. Victims also tend to be very quick to make excuses and to feel sorry for themselves. If you find yourself acting in this regard, you may want to ask yourself why. Chances are it's because you are attempting to avoid accepting the blame for something that has gone wrong. After all, who wants to take a hit to their self-esteem or think that they could be part of the problem?

By contrast, a player is what we all wish we were, in every situation. While being a victim can make us feel safe for the time being, taking on the role of a player ultimately makes us feel fulfilled because we know we are taking responsibility for the decisions we make. This in turn allows us to move forward with supreme confidence knowing that we have a choice and the power to change any circumstance that doesn't serve us.

Abundance vs. Scarcity

Another battle in the war within is a choice to see the world with a *scarcity mindset* or an *abundance mindset*. People with a scarcity mindset see the world and everything in it as finite. Life to them is a zero-sum game, meaning if someone else is winning, then they must be losing. They view everything as a pie with only so many slices to go around. They tend to take a very competitive approach with their peers and generally feel more pessimistic about the world around them.

On the other hand, individuals with an abundance mindset view the world as having enough for everyone. These people tend to have an outlook that is positive and optimistic. In the absence of the need to compete, they are free to collaborate with their peers and win-win relationships can be forged. A focus on abundance means that there are always more resources, money, and opportunities to be found or created.

Changing this part of your thinking might prove to be a bit challenging at first for an athlete who is coming from a place where the games themselves produce a winner and a loser. But once you start to see why this is so beneficial to you, you'll start to see things in a different way and realize that abundance is all around you.

Growth vs. Fixed

Choosing between a *growth mindset* and a *fixed mindset* is generally not a problem for athletes while they are in the arena. However, it can quickly become an issue and cause some substantial frustration as you try to step into a world or an environment that feels foreign to you. Luckily, athletes have coaches who are there to tell them that if they work hard they can improve. Athletes and coaches embody the growth mindset. They believe that challenges can be overcome with dedication and persistence. They see feedback (coaching) as a way to grow, and they focus on long-term goals instead of the short-term failures that they may be dealing with.

In contrast, a fixed mindset causes people to think that intelligence is fixed and that others are born with talent, so effort and persistence aren't worth it. To them, it's foolish to try when there is just no way to learn, adapt, develop new skills, or improve their chances of success. In fact, they might feel threatened by the success of others and may give up permanently if met with a temporary setback. They back away from challenges and often take feedback personally.

On Purpose vs. On Accident

How deliberate we are (or aren't) about our decisions can also tell us a lot about where our heads are. Why are you doing what you do? Are you making decisions based on the factors that are important to you or to someone else?

This was definitely a challenge for me, as I tried to shift from my playing days to a career. As I attempted to find the next thing, I generally went about it all wrong. I tended to look around to see what others were doing. If they seemed happy, maybe I needed to check out what they were doing. Then, maybe I'd be happy too. If they looked like they were making a nice salary, maybe that's where I needed to be. I was living my life on accident and spent far too many years doing things I didn't really care about. And because I didn't have a passion for what I was doing, I never reached my full potential in any of them.

Are you eating the cupcake because you feel it will add nutritional value to your body, or is it because it is sitting on the kitchen counter and you're bored? Did you choose to major in education in college because you felt like you were born to do that, or was it because your best friend wanted to be a teacher, and you didn't feel a strong calling to do anything else? Are you slowly working your way up to manager at your local hardware store because you are passionate about working in retail, or because it's familiar and easy? If you find yourself living on accident, it's never too late to start living on purpose.

LIMITING BELIEFS

You must identify and break through your personal ceilings in order to reach higher. You became good at pushing through your athletic limitations in your sport. But are there other limiting beliefs that reside inside your mind that you probably aren't even aware of? If you are frustrated and not sure who you are, now that you no longer compete as an athlete, you may be standing in your own way. Much more than any outside circumstance, we often hesitate to move in the direction that we want to go because there's a voice deep inside our mind that says *You can't have that,* or *That's out of your league.* It's embedded in your subconscious and has been living there comfortably for years. What is it, where did it come from, and more importantly, how do we kick it out of the stadium for good like a fan who's had a little too much Jack Daniels?

What are limiting beliefs anyway? They are thoughts that you believe to be true—whether they are actually true or not—that limit you in some way, shape, or form. Have you ever seen an athlete (maybe you were one of them) who worked to improve their speed by running with a harness strapped to their body and attached to a weighted sled at the other end? It's impossible to run at top speed with something heavy holding you back. That's what going through life with limiting beliefs feels like. Unlike this athlete who is using the harness and the weights to get better, the only purpose of limiting beliefs is to keep you from reaching your maximum potential. We can't let them win.

One of the biggest influences in shaping our beliefs about what's possible is our family. The people closest to you may have instilled beliefs in you (intentionally or unintentionally) that they learned when they were young and believed to be true. And so you may end up carrying these on in your own life.

Another source of our belief system is what we have learned in school. Whether the source was teachers or friends (who may have learned many beliefs from their families) they had an impact on what you believe to be true. When you have great trust and respect for the people in your life that you spend a great deal of time with, you are much more impressionable and inclined to accept what they are teaching you.

Finally, the things that happen to you and that you experience first-hand can have a big impact on what you accept as truth, especially if the experience is a negative one. For example, if you get a bad grade on a math test, you may conclude that you'll never be able to score well in that subject.

The most dangerous aspect of limiting beliefs is that they are very good at remaining hidden until we actively look for them. They may have been instilled in you long before you became an athlete and were never a problem while you were competing. But now it's important to pay attention to anything that may prevent you from moving forward confidently. They can be difficult to identify because how we think and the behaviors that come out of that thinking are our version of normal. It's just the way we have operated our entire lives. Below are several categories of the most common limiting beliefs.

Types Of Limiting Beliefs

Health

Now that you are no longer an athlete, you may find yourself making excuses about taking care of your body and your mind. You might believe that because you are no longer competing as an athlete, it's alright to let parts of your health slip. Be aware of whether you start to neglect the value of your health because you no longer see yourself and your physical attributes as valuable.

Money

Limiting beliefs around money keep many people from becoming as successful as they want to be. Negative beliefs about money can keep you playing small ball, cause you to self-sabotage, feel insecure, or fall into a negative mindset.

Self-Worth

Believing that you can't be great and achieve big things in anything outside the arena is the number one limiting belief that holds back athletes who have already accomplished so much in their respective sports.

Relationships

The challenge here is to understand that relationships don't operate successfully the way other parts of your life do. If you bring competition to the relationship, there will be rough waters ahead. Assess the relationship dynamics that you have observed in others around you. Finally, it's important to understand that your limiting beliefs in other areas may have an impact on your relationships with others.

Identify your limiting beliefs

1. Write down your beliefs

In the categories of health, money, self-worth, and relationships, write down your beliefs about each one. Write down several things you believe to be true under each topic. Try to be specific. Think about which beliefs may be holding you down and which ones are serving you well. Which beliefs do you agree with, and which ones do you want to let go of?

2. Write down your strong reactions

Are there situations where you have strong emotional reactions to things that are said or done? These are usually negative reactions to things you continue to struggle with more than once. For example, if you find yourself constantly struggling to communicate your thoughts and feelings with those close to you, you may have developed the belief that it's easier to avoid conflict than it is to initiate tough conversations.

FEAR

Finally, another important element of your mental game is overcoming fear. Fear wants to make you mediocre, to paralyze you, and to keep you from taking the steps and the risks that could lead to an amazing life. It can come in many forms such as resistance, anxiety, or even a deep-seated belief that you might actually attain what you want. When you get to a place where your biggest fear is the fear of regret, you'll know then that you are on the right track.

No one slips by fear without being noticed. Inside your former arena, you and fear weren't strangers. You knew each other well. Fear came with the territory. Fear was part of the price you paid to be an athlete. It was an expense that the observers on the sidelines weren't willing to incur.

You overcame many hurdles during your time on the inside. You had to overcome fears on a daily basis. The fear of playing a new position that you had no experience with in the past. Or a new technique that forces you to use your non-dominant hand to handle the ball. You, of course, experienced the fear of performing in front of others, putting yourself on display for the critics to judge you. Those are not small accomplishments. They are wins. Although no one keeps track of those types of stats, they might just be more important than the wins and losses. Battling fear as an athlete, not just on a daily basis, but often minute-by-minute is the game within the game. And it's a fight that the spectators can't see.

However, there is a light at the end of this fear tunnel. Because you are familiar with what it feels like to go a few rounds with fear, you can attack any newfound fears that might look different or go by a different name. It's time to dance with this new version of fear.

Feel the fear. Allow it to come into your living room and make itself comfortable on the couch. Ask it if it would like something to drink. Acknowledging not only that it exists but that it is welcome in your world will begin to alleviate the pressure that you would otherwise feel to run from it and avoid it at all costs.

Here's how to prevent this fear from hamstringing your future.

Identify your fear

Fear takes on many forms so it will be an advantage to you to point a finger at what type you are dealing with. Identifying the specific type will provide you with the first step of knowing your opponent's name. Given that you aren't the first to have fears surrounding this turning point in your life, let's focus on the two most common types of fears that athletes face when their careers end.

Fear of Uncertainty

We fear what we don't know. What will the next phase of your life look like now that your circumstances have been flipped upside down? Likely, everything about your current situation is different than it was before your retirement. Many of the questions you have about what's ahead simply can't be answered now.

No one will show up at your front door with a script for just how your life will play out in the coming days, months, and years. If they did, how would you feel about that? It would be the ultimate spoiler alert, wouldn't it? The reason spoiler alerts exist is to warn the people who don't want the plot to be spoiled. They want to experience the thrills that come with the uncertainty. If knowing how the movie ends was the point of it all, everyone would fast forward to the last ten minutes of the show. Where's the fun in that?

Embrace the drama. Welcome a little chaos. It might just get your blood pumping to think about the possibilities that could be hiding behind the fear of the unknown. While you can't navigate around the uncertainty, you can walk straight through it. Success is always on the other side of fear. What you fear most may just be the thing you most need to move toward.

Fear of Failure

Failure isn't an option. This is a mantra that I recited during at least one interview with the media during my playing days. Our team was coming off an average year, and we were expecting a big improvement in the upcoming season. What I was referring to was our team's strong desire to increase our win total from the year before and make it to a New Year's Day bowl game.

But failure can mean different things in different situations. Every elite performer, both in and out of the arena, has failed thousands of times. In many cases, they've failed way more than they've succeeded. And never are the two mutually exclusive. They complement each other.

Elon Musk, one of the richest men in the world, has had colossal failures along the road to the massive success and impact that he enjoys today. In 2000, he was removed from the company that he started, Paypal, while on his honeymoon. In 2006, he attempted his first rocket launch in his quest to make space travel accessible to everyone. The rocket exploded. In 2014, his electric car company, Tesla, had major problems with its batteries. Some versions of the Model S would catch fire spontaneously. That didn't stop Musk. His list of failures is quite long, but he is widely considered, even by his critics, a success.

So is failure an option? On the road to maximizing your full potential and determining the meaning at each stage of your journey, it better be.

Manipulate your fear

Once you've identified your fears, only then can you begin to leverage them to your own advantage. What separates the mediocre from the elite is the ability to adapt and use every resource available at the time to gain the upper hand.

Worst Case Scenario

What's the worst that could happen? In any new endeavor, because of the negativity bias, your mind goes immediately into protection mode. You assume that there will be problems. You use all the things that could go wrong to protect your ego and to reduce or eliminate the fear that you're overcome with.

But what if there was a way to disarm the fear to the point that it loses most of its strength? Try writing down the absolute worst possible future for yourself. Will you be homeless? Will you be completely alone without anyone who cares about you? Will you starve to death? Are you destined to be unhappy for the rest of your life? What is the likelihood of any of these questions? Slim to none. If the chances of the worst case actually happening are that tiny, then it begs the question, "How thin is the line between who I am and who I want to be?"

Manage Your Expectations

What does this mean? Usually, it means bringing your expectations down to a reasonable and realistic level. The phrase suggests that you don't get too excited or count on big things right away.

But isn't this exactly what fear hopes to do to you? To keep you in check, hold you down, and hold you back. Instead, reframe it. Fear is nothing more than information. It's feedback. Keep fear in its proper perspective and only give it the weight it needs, nothing more.

So feel the fear and do the thing anyway.

Stick Your Hand in the Fire

- Are you a player or a victim?
- Do you see the world as one of abundance or scarcity? How about your world?
- When faced with a new challenge, do you have a growth mindset or a fixed mindset?
- Will you live your life on purpose or on accident?
- What limiting beliefs from your past could potentially have a negative impact on your future?
- What do you fear the most?

"No one is going to beat you at being you."

—Naval Ravikant

5

IGNITE YOUR INFLUENCE

My fingerprints are not something I spend any time thinking about. While it's one of the most overlooked parts of our bodies, it's also one of the most fascinating. Of all the characteristics that we share with others, fingerprints aren't one of them. There are countless people inhabiting the earth that share the same eye color as you. You may even have the exact same name as another person. But your fingerprints belong only to you. (This amazing identifier is even more personal than DNA. Identical twins may share the same DNA but they don't have the same fingerprints.) The intricate patterns of loops, whirls, and arches that make up your unique fingerprints can't be claimed by anyone else on the planet. Only you.

How does that happen? How are these impressive marks formed in the first place? Scientists believe that during pregnancy, the basal layer of skin, which lies between the top layer and inner layer, undergoes some changes and begins to outgrow the other two. Because of the twisting, buckling, and folding of the basal layer, permanent marks are created. And because this process occurs differently for every fetus, no two patterns are alike.

Here's the best part: You had to *struggle* to create them. By moving inside the womb, you started to form your unique identity. By struggling and stretching, you shaped your place in the world of which you weren't yet a part. You put your mark on the world by establishing your exact position inside the womb. The fingerprints that exist on your hands right now were formed under pressure.

What does all this have to do with the transitioning out of the arena?

The meaning of life for you can only be realized *by you*. Only you can find the answer. Better yet, only you can *create* the answer. The individuality that you already possess sets you apart from every other human being on the planet. Let that sink in for a moment. Isn't it strange that the thing that makes you who you are, more than any other distinguishing trait, is something that you never think about? It's literally impossible to be exactly like anyone else. So why would you want to? You and your skin toiled, strained, and suffered to become who you are. It might be time to take responsibility for that fight.

With the realization of how you became one of one brings with it the notion that you can't be duplicated or replaced. And *that* brings with it a deep sense of responsibility. You don't just have the opportunity to take responsibility for your life, you must do it. No one can do it for you. No one can tell you or show you what your meaning will be. What lights the flame of responsibility? As Frankl wrote, "A man who becomes conscious of the responsibility he bears toward a human who affectionately waits for him, or to an unfinished work, will never be able to throw away his life."

YOUR SECRET WEAPON

When competing in the arena is no longer an option for you, you tend to feel as if you are just like everyone else. As an athlete, you stood out. You had something that made you unique. Your career was a gift, yes, but here's what it wasn't—a snapshot in time. Your uniqueness was *not* limited to your time in the arena.

Because I'm an introvert by nature, I tended to shy away from talking about my career after it ended. I didn't want to be seen as the sad athlete who was trying to cling to the stories and accomplishments from the glory days. To this day, I have a hard time being the first to mention a memory, game, or story from my past. Usually, friends and colleagues are the first to bring up my background while making a new introduction. I wanted to put the career and all its contents away. Hearing others recount or reminisce about old games only served as a reminder that I didn't have that life anymore. It twisted the knife deeper into the wound left by a promise unfulfilled.

But as time has gone by, I've realized that those stories and games bring people joy. Now, instead of downplaying them, they bring me joy as well. You are no longer striving to win games and using your physical gifts to stand out, but that doesn't mean that your career is now worthless. Instead, it's something to value. It's your unfair advantage. And if you can harness its powers, it can be your secret weapon.

You can use your past to ignite your future. Everything that you have gone through up to this point in your life can be viewed as an asset. You are standing on the precipice of one of the biggest opportunities of your life. It also will be one of the biggest challenges you'll face. If you consider for a moment and truly believe that your career is not something that you lost, you will begin to appreciate it as something you can use to experience victory in the future. Your playing days weren't something you merely endured or lived through, your career was something that was achieved. Although it happened in the past, its meaning will live on in the future.

What is your unfair advantage?

What if I told you that the key to everything that you want in the future is already inside of you? What if every minute of life that you've experienced so far has created something that only you possess? No other human being on the face of the earth has this thing. This force has been born out of every minute of your existence so far in this world. The city that you're from, who your parents are, what your interests are, the sport that you played, the school that you attended, the friends who you hung around with, the summation of your life as a whole. The combination of all your experiences including your wins, your losses, your thoughts, and your decisions, have all combined over the years to create something so unique, so one-of-a-kind, that only you know everything that is in there.

You've created a work of art through your experiences, triumphs, challenges, highs and lows, and reactions. Like your fingerprint, it separates you from every other living breathing human being on the planet. It's your *unfair advantage*. As it turns out, life isn't fair.

By examining seven key areas, you'll now begin to craft your unfair advantage so you can have a visual representation of exactly what you will bring to the table. This will not only assign meaning to your past but will also open up your mind to what can make you stand out in the future.

I suggest having a notebook, journal, or open document so you have a place to capture your thoughts. I'll specifically ask you to make a list of the elements of your unfair advantage.

CREATE YOUR UNFAIR ADVANTAGE

It's time to bring the story of you to life.

As we work through these key areas, I want you to pay special attention to the first two on the list. These are not only assets for your success, but they can be areas that trip up athletes the most. You want to be able to use your unfair advantage to its full capacity, not hide your authentic self.

Mistakes

It's tempting to only want to reveal the great wins, the achievements, and the finish lines crossed. You chased success as an athlete and to fall short was devastating at times. But a large part of what makes you who you are is your list of failures. It's where the gold is.

Every setback teaches a lesson. Your willingness to persevere beyond the losses and step into the arena again and again can be part of your unfair advantage. Not being ashamed of where you lost is a strength, not a weakness. So don't hold back. Know that failure is the best teacher.

So, as uncomfortable as it is to put your whole self out there, don't hide from the mistakes you've made. You owe them some credit for helping you bag some of your success.

ACTION: Write down two or three mistakes that taught you a valuable lesson or impacted who you are in some way.

Achievements

Talking about yourself and your achievements in front of others may feel like you are bragging. It might seem as though others won't want to hear you acknowledge the great things that you've done. You may think that you are being considerate of others and their egos by staying quiet. In reality, the opposite is true.

Who is benefiting from you staying small? Certainly not you. Why should you be ashamed about what you've been through? How much time, effort and commitment did you invest in your career? You should be proud of all of it. The good, the bad, and everything in between.

Shrinking also doesn't benefit those that you think you could be protecting. Hearing you speak about yourself may just give them permission to think about and use their own unfair advantage.

ACTION: Write down two or three achievements that you sometimes shrink away from or avoid talking about.

Talent

Though it may not be obvious to you yet, your talents extend beyond the world of sports. Everyone has unique talents that they were born with that they use on a daily basis. Because they are so familiar, though, they may not register as talents. These are traits that come easily to you without mustering up much energy or investing a ton of time. They come naturally to you but are a struggle for others.

You may have the talent of emotional intelligence which allows you to recognize when someone is feeling uncomfortable in a group setting. Maybe you have an amazing ability to remember important dates and events from the past or do complex math in your head. You might be skilled with your hands, great with kids, comfortable speaking in front of people, or analyzing financial information. Whatever it is, you've got something that is a huge component of your unfair advantage.

ACTION: *Write down at least two or three talents that you inherently possess. This may be challenging at first because, again, what seems natural to you might not initially seem like a talent. If you're having any trouble, ask family and friends what talents they recognize in you. Another approach is to start paying attention to what others ask you for help with.*

Character

Your character has been developed over the course of your entire life. It's been influenced by your environment, what you've been taught, and the people you've been exposed to. Your family and friends have had a big influence on your character as well. All the good and the bad have contributed to the person you are today, including the things you stand for and the values you are passionate about.

Are you rational, honest, loyal? How do you treat other people, and does it change depending on who they are? How do you respond to various situations? Once again, these are so ingrained in you and make up the core of who you are so much that it can be difficult at first to assess yourself. If you struggle, ask for feedback from others.

ACTION: *List at least two or three character traits that are unique to you. Think of the traits that you admire in others. These most likely are traits that you admire in yourself or aspire to embody in the future.*

Experience

Your experience makes up the most important part of your unfair advantage. Most people have not experienced the things that you have. As we have discussed, you've lived through challenges that few have had the opportunity to endure, either because of lack of ability, opportunity, or willingness. And as a result, you've gone through things that have caused others to admire what you've been through.

More significant than your experiences are the lessons and skills that you've acquired as a result. These takeaways alone can separate you from the rest of the pack.

ACTION: List at least two or three experiences that you've lived through in the last several years. Feel free to add a note about what you learned from those experiences too.

Connections

The people with whom you've connected and built relationships in your life might have the biggest impact on your unfair advantage. Why? They have come to know you and more importantly, trust you. The exact combination of people you know will bring tremendous value to you in the future if you work to develop your network the same way you cultivated your abilities in the sports world.

Keep in mind that as an athlete, you may have lived in the public eye to some extent. This means that there may be people who you don't know but who do know you. This, in turn, could make it easier to expand and grow your network if you are strategic about it. Regardless of how big it is, your network is made up of strong bonds and people who want to see you succeed.

ACTION: Write down at least two or three influential people in your life that you could work to develop a symbiotic and strong relationship with over the next several months or years.

Knowledge

Over the years, you've gathered more knowledge than you realize. Classes in school, documentaries that you've watched, or stories from a wise relative have all contributed to your own personal library of knowledge. Don't make the mistake of taking this for granted. It can be easy to assume that everyone knows what you do. But most knowledge is not common. It is specialized and customized to how you process and perceive it. Even two people who learn the exact same thing might interpret it in totally different ways.

What are you curious about? What questions motivate you to seek out answers? Are there areas of education that are attractive to you that may seem a little weird to almost everyone else? What you've learned may seem uncommon and special to others.

(I personally have allocated a ridiculous amount of space in my brain and accumulated too much useless information on pop culture from my younger days, including movie quotes and connecting names of songs with the artists who sang them.)

ACTION: *Take a few minutes to write out at least two or three things that you are knowledgeable about. These items don't have to relate to one another or seem significant right now.*

You should have roughly ten to twenty items to use and work with. Now that you have laid the foundation for your unfair advantage, it's time to take it one step further and lean in a little more to distill what you've learned into a clear picture of who you are now.

LEAN INTO YOUR UNFAIR ADVANTAGE

What are the patterns or trends that start to emerge from the picture of not only your career inside the arena but from your life as a whole? The answers will come. But first, you will need to ask a few more detailed questions. This process will distinguish you from every other athlete whose journey may have been similar to yours, but after closer examination, is quite different.

Your greatest hit

Who is your favorite musical artist? Can you name their greatest hit single? Of course you can because you're a huge fan. So what is *your* greatest hit? Can your biggest fans name it? Can you?

My biggest hit was produced on November 7th, 1998, in Columbus, Ohio. I was fortunate to be a part of the Michigan State team that went on the road and upset the #1 ranked Ohio State Buckeyes. Coming into that game, we were unranked and were an unfocused 4-4 squad. We were 28-point underdogs coming into the game, and no one outside of the program believed we could pull off the win, especially since this wasn't an early-season game.

Sometimes teams ranked high at the beginning of the season fall off after a few weeks and end up sliding down the list of top teams as the season progresses. Everyone knew that this year's Ohio State was built differently. They had been picked by many analysts at the beginning of the season to win it all. And now that we were entering the eighth week of the season, those predictions only seemed like more of a lock. Ohio State was undefeated and featured several future first-round NFL draft picks.

Despite falling behind 24-9 in the third quarter after I threw a costly interception that was returned for a touchdown, we went on to an unbelievable comeback, upsetting the Buckeyes 28-24 in their own arena. I now have family members that live in the Columbus area and, although the Buckeyes have since won a national championship, that game is still referred to by many Ohio State fans as "Black Saturday."

What's your greatest hit?

Biggest flop

Sometimes the higher you aim, the greater the risk of falling flat on your face. What did that look like in your world? Maybe it was a mental blunder when the game was on the line or maybe it was something like an injury that was out of your control. While devastating at the time, this moment no doubt served to make you stronger and more resilient. What was the one lowest moment that shaped you into who you are today?

For me, I was benched during my last home game as a collegiate player. In front of the home crowd, and in front of my family, I was told to have a seat. Granted, I was still nursing an injury and had thrown an interception in what was the most important game of the year. There was a New Year's Day bowl game on the line, something that hadn't been achieved by the program in almost twenty years. But the hardest part of the situation was that once my backup came into the game, there was not another pass play called the rest of the way. I could've easily handed the ball off without an issue. We hung on to beat Penn State and finish the regular season 9-2, the best season in over a decade.

In the locker room after the game and surrounded by 100 teammates and coaches who were celebrating the win, I never felt more alone. I felt sorry for myself, and I was angry. I quickly showered up, grabbed my stuff, and headed out of the stadium. I went back to my apartment, didn't take calls, and just wanted to be alone. I could have searched for the meaning at that moment.

Instead, I was wrapped up in myself and my interests. When I think about that day, my mind goes not to the win or even the fact that I got pulled from the game, but to how I chose to handle the situation.

What has been the moment that you wish you could erase from history?

Biggest takeaway

The feelings of nausea were not going away. What was once fun wasn't anymore. After returning home from football practice one evening as a ten-year-old, I announced to my parents that I wanted to quit the team. They were shocked, to say the least. They of course asked what the reason was and after I offered something lame about not liking it anymore, they began to give me a list of reasons why I shouldn't quit. They reminded me about how much I had loved the game and how others had remarked to them about my talent, even at a young age. After some back and forth, they realized that I wasn't going to change my mind or give them the real reason for wanting to hang up my cleats and shoulder pads and call it a career.

The truth was that the coach of our team had a deep, booming, scary voice and screamed for the entire practice. And he screamed directly at me when trying to make his point. That might not sound that bad, but to a kid who had never been exposed to that before, I wasn't exactly dying to get to practice every evening. What was once something that I looked forward to now became something that was causing an unpleasant physical reaction every day. I still loved the game, and I wasn't sure what the future had in store for me; I just knew that I wanted out. But what would my parents think? What would they say? What would my teammates say at school the next day after not seeing me at practice and hearing that I had quit? I didn't have time to think about any of that. I just wanted to be done.

My mom, who somehow instinctively knew exactly how to handle a situation she had never faced herself, paused for a second and informed me that if I wanted to give up football, that would be fine. And, for a split second, I felt a huge sense of relief. But she quickly added that because the current season was already half over, I'd have to finish what I started and complete the current year with my team. I had no choice but to agree and proceeded to immediately dread the next day's practice.

My mentality improved, though. Things got better, and I finished the rest of the season with my team. After that little hiccup, I never looked back and was the first one to register to play every fall until my career ended.

What's one overarching theme or lesson did you take away from being an athlete?

Fork in the road

There are defining moments in every life. Big decisions that need to be made at crucial times. The bigger the decision, the more difficult it usually is to make. The reason for that can be twofold. First, the two choices sometimes are less than favorable. You might not want either one. Second, you just can never know up front if you're making the right one.

During my sophomore year in college, I began to face chronic and excruciating back pain. For an athlete whose job it is to twist their torso to throw a ball hundreds of times a day, this presented a problem. The pain prevented me from practicing and playing at times, and I traveled around the eastern half of the country visiting some of the best doctors to help figure out the problem. There were evaluations, tests, scans, and injections with six-inch spinal needles. And still no concrete answers.

I was sent to a sports psychologist to see if he could help with the dejection I was feeling, and he did help me somewhat. But after my junior year, which was filled with the still lingering physical pain along with the emotional pressure that comes with barely hanging on to my starting job, I began to seriously consider calling it a career and not returning for my senior season.

Maybe I just didn't have the courage to tell my coaches, teammates, and parents that I wanted to walk away. But I now realize that it wasn't the fear of what others would think of me, it was the fear of what I would've thought of myself. Had I chosen to walk away with only one guaranteed year left to play the game I had always loved, I would've missed out on some of the greatest memories of my entire life: beating our arch-rival Michigan, beating Notre Dame in their house, breaking school records, and helping our team beat Florida on a last-second field goal in the 2000 Citrus Bowl to finish the season ranked #7 in the country.

After my junior season at Michigan State, I was honored by our coaching staff with the team award for perseverance at our team's annual end-of-the-year banquet. This was a result of my previously-mentioned back troubles, among other things. I had learned the value of perseverance as a ten-year-old and it came full circle over a decade later. The beauty of sports is that it provides so many lessons along the way.

When did you come to your fork in the road?

USE IT OR LOSE IT

Unlike in the billion-dollar sports trading card industry, there wasn't a single duplicate of you produced.

Now that you've thought through and identified the components of your unfair advantage, it's time to deploy it. First, to bring anything to life, you must first give it a name. Nothing is real in your mind unless it has a name. Don't worry, giving your unfair advantage a name won't mean that you'll need to broadcast it to everyone you come across. Because showing is always better than telling, you'll have a much greater impact by exhibiting the traits that make up your unfair advantage. Since you've done the hard work of figuring out your unfair advantage and putting it on paper, your self-awareness has already improved. And so will your confidence.

It's also important to know that, in a way, we are all in sales. Even if your current role doesn't have a title related to sales or if you recoil at the mere thought of trying to persuade anyone to do anything, you work in the sales department of *You, Inc.*

Whether it's selling your significant other on why you should have tacos for dinner or whether it's pitching your coworkers on your idea for a new format for office meetings, you're always selling something. This becomes clear when you become a parent. I am constantly selling (begging) my two kids on why they should pick their clothes up off the floor. And they, in turn, try to sell me on why they shouldn't.

What might using your unfair advantage look like? Are there patterns or trends that have emerged after reading this chapter? Begin to think about how you can start applying what you've learned to your work, job, or business. Maybe you have a big interview on the horizon or you've got your eye on your dream job. In what ways can you use what you have to reach those goals?

Have you discovered that you have the ability to stay calm in stressful situations? How could this benefit your relationships? Could you use this ability to help a family member who panics when things go off track?

As you know by now, adversity is part of the game of life and is always threatening to deter you from reaching your full potential.

Can you apply your unfair advantage to reduce the impact adversity has on you? Can you use it to limit your suffering or someone else's?

Go all in on you. Double down on your unfair advantage. As an athlete, you worked tirelessly on improving your weaknesses. And I'm not going to pretend that you shouldn't try to improve parts of yourself that need some work. But the surest path to fulfillment and meaning is to recognize the gifts you have been given and to use them to the best of your ability.

Just do it. When you see those three words together, you know immediately what message they represent. Inspiration to athletes all over the world. Nike, the iconic athletic brand that outfits athletes and non-athletes everywhere with its shoes and apparel has been telling their story to the world for over a half-century. Phil Knight, the founder of Nike, and a couple of co-workers named the company after Nike, the Greek goddess of victory.

Nike was best known as Zeus' divine charioteer. Often in the possession of golden-winged sandals and the staff of Hermes, Nike would circle the battlefield, giving praise and adulation to the victors during the Titanomachy, a series of wars in Greek mythology.

Nike's greatest strengths were speed and agility. In some ancient texts, she was known to possess massive amounts of strength as well. But it was her sheer speed and her large wings that allowed her to hover over battlefields, watch the struggle unfold below, and then reward the victors with fame and honor. These attributes set her apart. Not only was she physically gifted, but she was also able to bring others who had accomplished great things to the forefront and praise them for their efforts. This is what she was known for.

What do you want to be known for now that your time in the sports world as an athlete is over? The answer to that is most likely found in recognizing and leaning into your unfair advantage.

Stick Your Hand in the Fire

- What is your greatest hit?
- What is your biggest flop?
- Your biggest takeaway?
- What was your fork in the road?

"The pen that writes your life story must be held in your own hand."

—Dr. Irene C. Kassorla

6

THE BURNING QUESTION

Now that you are better equipped with the knowledge that you are and can be much more than your athletic career (or even the work that you do), it's time to distinguish between two questions. The wrong question will lead in the wrong direction. The *burning question* will open up a world of possibilities to you.

You'll no doubt be asked the wrong question by others around you. More often, you'll ask this wrong question of yourself. Along with this question, there will be a multitude of things that will try to distract you from the question you should be asking of yourself. And you'll have to know how to make sense of it all.

Unfortunately, meaning in our lives won't just appear. It won't announce that it has arrived. It doesn't tap you on the shoulder and wave. The burning question is the key to unlocking the realm of possibilities that await you. It opens a door that hides behind it a room full of more doors. How do you determine which door is the right one once inside? That's not important right now; we will get to that later. The first step is unlocking the main door so you have access to all the other ones.

This burning question will be one of the most important questions you are ever asked. The answer, or more specifically, the *answers* will be critical to the process of beginning to move toward a life of meaning and significance.

Before we dig deep into what this question is and how it moves us toward finding meaning, we need to tackle some of the obstacles that will keep you asking the wrong question.

EXISTENTIAL VACUUM

One of the biggest challenges that you will face on the road to a life of meaning and reaching your full potential is a phenomenon known as the *existential vacuum*.

Aimless. Empty. Drifting. No sense of direction. Have you experienced any of these since your playing days ended? You can't go back, but paralysis prevents you from moving forward. Sound familiar?

My football career fulfilled me even in ways that I still haven't completely come to understand. Victor Frankl's book, though, provided the basis for the meaning that being an athlete gave me and the negative feelings that I would experience when my career ended. His words gave me a way to at least attach a name to what I was feeling. He identified the feelings of emptiness as the "existential vacuum." It's that sense that something should be happening but isn't. It's a feeling that life could and should be more exciting, more fun, and more rewarding. But it isn't.

The existential vacuum is where I lived when my career ended, though I didn't know that I was there. I felt like something was off, but I didn't know how dangerous that place could be. The worst part was not knowing how to get out.

Easily accessible and open to the public, the existential vacuum is an easy place to find. Admission is free. In fact, I believe this is where most athletes go when their career ends. This is where pleasure makes its home. While it's easy to get into, it can feel almost impossible to get out of. Why is it a dangerous place to be? Because pleasure does not equal meaning.

Remember where Frankl said meaning could be found? (see Chapter 3). During my time at Michigan State, I was performing and striving toward creating a body of work. I was striving not just for myself but for my teammates and every Spartan athlete that had come before me. And I was taught to welcome adversity with a positive attitude. *Work*, *relationships*, and *suffering* were present and interconnected elements. If only I had known at the time what I was experiencing and why I was experiencing it.

It took me years to discover that, when any of these elements were taken away, the sense of meaning started to fade, and I would slide back into the existential vacuum. Meaning doesn't mingle with just one or two of the components. It needs all three.

Meaning matters. But it doesn't last forever. Careers come to an end. Amusement parks close. Musicians sing their last song.

Apathy is the enemy

Enemies are evil. Enemies want you to feel fear. Enemies want you to lose hope. They want you to freeze. They want you to give up emotionally. When you're fumbling through the dark without a flashlight and you're looking for the way out of the state of mind that you've found yourself in, that's when the enemy comes out of nowhere to introduce himself. You will be presented with a buffet of emotions when your career ends. All of which deserve some attention and can help you understand and assess your current situation. Most will serve you in a positive way. Apathy, however, will lock you up and throw away the key.

Apathy is defined as a lack of interest, concern, feeling, or emotion. With any big change on the horizon, there is a tendency to experience one of two default emotions.

The first is a sense of being overwhelmed. You closed one big chapter of your life and now are faced with the magnitude of what happens next. There's pressure to not only figure it out but to make those decisions quickly. Don't succumb to it.

The second is a sense that anything you encounter in the future won't have the same stimulating effect that sports did. This leaves you with sensations of being underwhelmed at the prospect of going out to hunt for meaning in your life.

Both can cause your internal protection mechanisms to shut your systems down. This can also leave you feeling indifferent, not only to positive emotions like joy and excitement but also to anger and frustration.

Apathy's venom can steal your motivation slowly and methodically. It may begin by skipping an offer by a friend to hang out. Next, it could have you talking yourself out of a workout and asking "What's the point?" Eventually, you could be going out of your way to not do things that you used to enjoy. The danger with apathy is that it tempts you with comfort and ease. Which is the opposite of why you excelled inside the arena.

On the inside, you cared deeply. You cared so much, you were willing to stick your hand in the fire day in and day out without being promised anything for your efforts. So where's the meaning in *not caring*?

When my career ended, I tried to convince myself that I was all right with it all coming to a halt. I tried to put everything that I had invested emotionally into the sport I loved on a shelf in a closet. I boxed up the trophies, plaques, and jerseys, left them in the storage room, and turned out the lights. I *acted* like I didn't care. I thought that if I distanced myself from sports and made people believe that

I was more than an athlete, they would believe it. But I didn't believe it, so how could they?

When you feel yourself not caring, look for a way to give yourself a quick win. Find something small to care about. Shovel the snow off the steps. Crack open a book about how Steve Jobs built Apple. And above all else, tell yourself the truth. If you are telling yourself lies, take responsibility for that. Own it. You're going to make mistakes. Recover quickly. If you're telling yourself that you don't care or acting like you don't in front of others to hide your discomfort, you're just confused about the next steps. There's no room for apathy in your arsenal.

Every enemy will try to outwit you and make it as easy as possible to defeat you with very little effort on their part. They'll dig a deep hole and cover it with leaves and branches hoping you don't notice as you approach it with your pupils dilated and your head on a swivel.

In addition to the apathy found in the existential vacuum, there are several other traps a former athlete can fall victim to. We are going to look at two of the most common ones to beware of.

TWO SURVIVAL TRAPS

One of the most devastating mistakes you as a former athlete can make is allowing external factors to determine your path to meaning. What do I mean? Uncertainty over the lack of direction in your life may lead you to make some desperate choices that might not be in your best interests. These traps are so common they aren't exclusive to athletes and their journey to find meaning. These pitfalls are treacherous and tempting because they call out to our need to stick with a tribe. Any tribe.

In the fight to survive in the immediate aftermath of your playing days coming to an end, you may feel the urge to find something to do. Without the necessary time and effort spent on asking yourself deeper questions like the ones in this book, you may find yourself in a state of urgency. The voice calling you to do *something* and find *something* may be ringing loudly in your brain. And given this somewhat panicked state, too many of us fall victim to what I like to call the two Temptation Traps.

Trap #1: What others are doing

You are a unique collection of ideas, talents, and DNA. The tendency, though, for so many retired athletes—who don't have a clear picture of who they are or the power they possess—is to start down a path that isn't the one meant for them. So they look to others for direction, looking for a clue as to what might be working for others. Seems like the logical thing to do. They start asking, "Who seems happy in their chosen path?" and "Who makes a lot of money?"

Through conversations that you'll likely be having or already have had, you may hear the excitement in the voices of friends who seem to have it all figured out. They'll tell you about their training, the people that they are meeting, the benefits package that comes with the job, or how their year in Europe is going to be fantastic.

Tim Tebow gained popularity during his college career at the University of Florida, where he won the Heisman Trophy and led his team to two national championships. As he transitioned to the professional level, Tebow faced immense pressure to conform to the traditional pocket passing style of quarterbacking that was favored by NFL teams at that time. However, Tebow was known for his unorthodox style of play, characterized by his running ability and propensity for making plays outside the pocket.

As a member of the Denver Broncos in 2011, with the team off to a lackluster start, Tebow was given a chance to start as the team's quarterback. In a daring move, he decided to embrace his unique style of play, which involved more running, improvisation, and unconventional passes. Tebow's choice to stray from the traditional mold and focus on his strengths attracted significant attention and polarized opinions. Despite experiencing skepticism and criticism, he led the Broncos to a series of dramatic come-from-behind victories. His success sparked the phenomenon known as Tebow Mania, with fans fervently supporting his unorthodox playing style.

However, as the pressure mounted and scrutiny intensified, Tebow's success was short-lived. Following a playoff loss during the 2011 season, the Broncos signed Peyton Manning, a highly accomplished pocket passer, as their new quarterback, forcing Tebow to adapt to a more conventional style. Consequently, Tebow's performance declined, and he struggled to find a long-term place in the NFL.

Looking back, Tebow admitted in interviews that he regretted conforming to the traditional quarterback style when he had initially succeeded by embracing his individuality. He expressed frustration and felt internal pressure to change and believed that he would have achieved more had he stuck to his unique playing style, which had originally endeared him to fans and brought him success.

Tim Tebow's story serves as a cautionary tale of an athlete who temporarily abandons his true self to do what others are doing, only to later regret not staying true to his individuality and strengths. This, of course, applies just as much outside of the arena.

Trap #2: What others think you should do

The second common trap that I've seen many retired athletes fall into is selecting an option or options that someone else thinks you should choose. Those who love you and care about you want you to be happy and think they know you best. So they offer to help in any way they can. Sometimes it can be beneficial to gain an outside perspective on your situation, and there are times when soliciting outside advice can be helpful.

But there can be risk involved in placing too much stock in what others want you to do or think you should do. While they may know you very well, they don't walk in your shoes. As confident as you may have been in the arena, you could find yourself doubting your own instincts and instead trusting the voice of someone who may not have to live with the decisions that you make.

As lonely and unsettling as these times can be, the frustration that you may be feeling is actually a good thing. It can mean that, again, you care and you're applying pressure to something that's important to you. Your search is unique to you and the mystery of what will be can only be solved by you.

My wife Christina has some very redeeming qualities. Not just in my eyes but in the eyes of others who know her, even complete strangers. She has this special way of making you feel important when you are in her presence and because of that, people naturally gravitate toward her. Generally, people like to talk about themselves, and my wife gives them every opportunity to do just that, all while giving them constant affirmation throughout the entire conversation. As a result, she's like a magnet. I can't count the times that the two of us have been in the middle of a conversation in public and someone who knows her will walk up and just start talking to her as if I'm not even there.

When Christina was in high school and coaching some kids at a youth camp, some of the adult teachers and advisors commented on how good she was with the children. They even suggested that she might one day become a teacher. She filed the comments away and went off to college. Not unlike a lot of incoming college freshmen, athletes or not, she didn't have a concrete idea of what she was there to study. After the first year of general prerequisites, and after a friend also suggested that she'd be a good teacher, she made education her major.

Twenty years later, she is wishing that she had been more intentional with this big decision. She has regrets about what she chose to do professionally and who she became. Of course, there are several factors that can contribute to these big forks in the road and the responsibility of our choices ultimately falls upon our own shoulders, but you can see how easy it can be to get trapped.

You may be thinking that if you start down a path that you discover isn't for you, it's possible to change course. And I couldn't agree more that you can and should if you feel that's what you need to do. But as life continues to unfold, things can get more and more complicated. Families are started, promotions at work are received, and the pressure to stay on the safe path can get built up making it harder to make a bold move in a new direction.

Part of the magic of our journey is that it is ours. It's ours to struggle with, to agonize over, and to be proud of. No one can do this important work of making meaning for us. Not even the ones who love us the most, who often ask us the wrong question. Our growth and progress rely instead on asking ourselves the right question: The Burning Question.

QUESTION THIS, NOT THAT

One question can change your life. If it's the right one. It can create new opportunities and take your future in directions that you didn't know existed. The key is to start the habit of asking questions. The more you ask, the more answers you will receive. And the more answers you get, the better the answers will be.

As an athlete, though, there is an enormous distinction between the question you are asking yourself and the one that you *should* be asking instead. The wrong question is so common and used so frequently that we never slow down to examine it further and ask ourselves what it really means.

We are a society that bases our identity and how we see ourselves around what we do to earn a living. Consider the last party that you attended. When you meet someone new, the conversation usually starts with an exchange of names and a handshake. Next, someone inevitably asks "What do you do?" When so much of our time is devoted to doing things that fall into the category of "work," it's understandable that that's where the questions lead. Often all it takes is swapping out a couple of words from the wrong question to change the way you now view the problem and the potential answers. And that can be exciting. It can bring hope and it can change your perspective in an instant.

What should I do?

The natural question to ask yourself when your career ends is "What should I do?" What should you fill the void left by your sport with? Practice time, games, training, and everything that comes with being an athlete is now gone. These are things you "did."

Let's take a closer look at the words in the question itself. The word *what* signifies work. Things, activities, and skills that you possess or achieve. The word *should* is where I think this question gets interesting. The word brings with it a feeling of expectation. As if there's a predefined answer and you just haven't realized it yet. That sense of expectation can come from friends and family, society as a whole, or from within yourself. Whose expectations for your future do you care about? Whose expectations matter the most? Yours do.

Finally, the word *do* again reinforces your career, vocation, or what you do to earn money. Now with so much extra time on your hands, it's easy to see how your focus can quickly shift to figuring out what to do next. After all, your sport and the time you devoted to it shaped your identity to a large extent.

The question *What should I do?* only addresses one-third of the ways in which you can find meaning in your life. (It focuses on work, ignoring relationships and suffering.) Asking only this question of yourself paints a backward picture. It puts "what you do" at the center of an imaginary wheel, with spokes extending out to try to connect all the other parts of your life. We can be much more than what we *do*, though. To get there, we must ask a better question.

Who could I become?

So how do you even begin down the road to meaning? Where do you start? If it all sounds a bit overwhelming, don't worry. There is a question that you can ask yourself that will get the creative juices flowing and start to turn your attention away from what you've lost and redirect your focus to the future. The burning question is *Who could I become?* Say it out loud.

Breaking down the words in the question once again is a helpful exercise. Right off the bat, the word *who* signifies a person, not a job or any activity. It directs your attention to the individual on a much more intimate, more all-encompassing level. Humans are complex, and athletes are no different. The word *could* is only different than *should* by one letter but is worlds away in terms of what it can mean for your thought process as you start to ask yourself these questions. *Could* beams with excitement because of the possibilities it offers. There is limitless potential in that five-letter word.

That leaves the last but most important word: *become*. This word indicates the fact that you are always changing and evolving. It lets you understand that it's okay to not be a complete product at the present moment. It also alludes to the idea that there is a process of discovery still ahead.

> The burning question is
> *Who COULD I become?*

Let's go back to the party example. What if instead of asking strangers "What do you do?" everyone asked each other "Who are you becoming?" How would that change things? It would force you to take a look at the other parts of your life that usually get pushed to the back burner. If you ask that question to the next person you meet at any social function, you will instantly become the most interesting person they meet that day, and you will have certainly left a lasting impression on them. Who knows where the answers they come up with will lead?

SELF-EDUCATION

With apologies to my professors at Michigan State, the majority of my education in college came by way of my time on the football field. The tough love, the critical feedback, learning to handle adversity, resilience, and so many other lessons that equipped me to deal with life outside the arena were all learned by being in the fire, not in a classroom. While I'm beyond grateful for those lessons because I still continue to access and rely on them constantly, the education they gave me wasn't sufficient to answer the burning question for myself.

When my time inside the arena ended, it didn't take long to realize I needed more. To figure out *who I should become*, I needed to understand what was out there, what had been done before, and by whom. I needed to start to formulate my future self. To do that, I needed an education.

Instead of a traditional degree or program, though, I needed a *self-education*, one that I could direct and control. A series of lessons that I could curate for myself and use to follow what felt exciting to me. Warren Buffett, one of the richest and most well-known businessmen in the world, renowned for his savvy and uber-success in the world of investments, thinks "the best investment you can make is in yourself."

Who you could become is more than a reflective question that you ask of yourself. Pondering the question implies that you need to take action and seek out the answer if you truly want to transform.

Curiosity as currency

We were all born with a curious mind. As kids, you asked questions about everything and wanted to understand why things were happening as they were. You badgered your parents with the need to know why the sky was blue and the grass was green. But as the years passed and you slowly gained more knowledge, you became less and less curious about the world around you. You took on a more comfortable expert role. You became more sure of your own opinions and quicker to explain rather than ask about them.

The key ingredient in self-education is curiosity. The intention to be actively curious is crucial in the pursuit to grow and become your best self. If that intention is not set and pursued, your perspectives and thoughts aren't stretched and knowledge will start to plateau.

Aside from learning new things, there is also another benefit of setting an intention of curiosity. It can be used as currency. As Dale Carnegie wrote in his book, *How to Win Friends and Influence People*, "To be interesting, be interested." Interested in life, in people, in ideas. Interested in the successes and failures of the people you meet and interact with. You can learn something new from everyone. And that thing might just have a significant impact on your future. In exchange for giving you their opinions, perspectives, and stories, you also give them something in return. And that something is a genuine interest in them.

People inherently love to talk about themselves. When you are interested, it naturally makes you more attractive to the other person. This in turn deepens relationships and makes you memorable in their minds. You get wisdom or at least entertainment, and they get to tell you their story or the satisfaction of passing what they've learned on to you. Everybody wins. And you both might get the added bonus of developing a bond that continues in the years to come. You can gain from others and simultaneously form new thoughts about who you could become, what you agree with, and what you don't.

Listen intently, observe, and ask thoughtful questions. Adopt a beginner's mind, strive to find new ways of doing things, and never stop questioning how something could be improved upon in some way.

Your belief system was programmed into you. If you don't like parts of that system, did you know that you can "rewire" your brain? Have you ever heard of *neuroplasticity*? Many years ago, scientists believed that our brains stopped developing in adulthood. They believed that only during childhood was the brain able to be shaped and developed. However recent research in the last half-century or so shows that the brain is a dynamic organ. It can be influenced and shaped by various types of mental stimulation as well as physical activity. Your brain can literally change size and shape as a result of decisions that you make about what to put into it. How cool is that?

So if you have a limiting belief (or many), you have the ability to do something about it. You can change it for the better. And this just doesn't work on limiting beliefs, you can use this knowledge to seriously affect your future. While there will always be factors at play in your life that are unavoidable or influenced by outside forces, you are in control of your future and your happiness. How do we do that? Rewiring your brain may sound like a complicated and difficult pursuit, but it's really much simpler than you might think.

Considering who you could become can be the result of some very simple, yet powerful intentions you pursue on a regular basis to stretch your brain, keep it active, and upgrade your brain's software. There are countless ways to ignite some small brain flames, but here are a few places to start. These will not only rewire the circuitry inside your brain but could get you excited about the possibilities that await you.

Books

Developing a reading habit is one of the best things you can do for your future. Not only do you expose yourself to new ideas and possibilities, but research has shown that it may also help you live longer. One study at Yale University showed that compared to non-readers, book readers had a 23-month survival advantage.

Need a list? Grab your free copy of "10 Books That Will Change The Way You Think" here: **outsidethearena.com/10books**

Podcasts

Like mini-audiobooks, podcasts cover just about every topic you could possibly be curious about. From personal development to pop culture to weird history to sports, there is something for every interest. Gain knowledge through your headphones as you work out or are driving to get that smoothie.

Learn a New Skill

Tackle learning a new language or musical instrument. Take an online course (many are free!) or subscribe to a YouTube channel where someone is teaching a new skill.

Volunteer

Getting involved in an organization or event that serves others will not only get you to think beyond your own circumstances, but you may make valuable connections with people who can open new worlds for you. You may discover new opportunities in your community you didn't know about or new ways to serve others.

The question of who you could become invites a world of possibilities into your brain if you are willing to not place any limitations on the answers.

Stick Your Hand in the Fire

- Have you been tempted to follow someone else's path even though it doesn't feel aligned with what excites you?
- Have you struggled with structure now that your playing days are over?
- What immediately comes to mind when you ask yourself the burning question "Who could I become?"

R

Part Three

RELENTLESS ACTION

Every year, there are 16,405,000 flights that pierce the sky over the United States. These planes carry people eager to travel to other states to visit relatives that they haven't seen in years. The metal birds transport families who are excited to start the tropical vacation they planned months earlier. There are mountains to discover, historical places to learn from, and business meetings to attend. There are even sporting events to compete in. Millions of annual passengers drive to the airport, check their luggage, shuffle through security, and board the plane without marveling at what is about to happen.

Because two brothers from Ohio were intrigued by a helicopter toy they were given as children, all of us now have the luxury of getting from one place to another in a matter of hours instead of days by stepping onto an airplane.

Orville and Wilbur Wright were fascinated by how things worked. Curious and ambitious, they began their journey of etching their names into the history books by jumping into the printing business. Next, they opened a bicycle shop. But their love of flight never faded, and they began what would eventually lead to being credited with inventing one of the most transformational advances in human history.

Although the outcome was monumental, the path to get there was filled with more than just the dream of one day seeing an aircraft lifted from the earth by a pilot and carrying happy passengers. Like the engine that powers the flight, the brothers needed to bring something to their vision that would get it off the ground: action. Not just any type of action but the kind that doesn't stop. Unfazed, unflappable, and unconcerned with what could go wrong. They moved forward and operated with consistency and persevered in spite of failed attempts to get their designs into the air. They were relentless.

They first built gliders in their bicycle shop. They made the long trip to Kitty Hawk North Carolina to test their prototypes on beaches with strong ocean winds as well as sand to provide a soft landing spot. The location provided an ideal environment for learning and experimenting.

They spent countless hours observing the behavior of birds so they could apply what they learned to their inventions. They weren't just imagining. They were *doing*. Orville Wright once said, "The airplane stays up because it doesn't have the time to fall." He probably was referring to the literal and technical aspects of flight, but I can't help seeing these words as a transcendent piece of wisdom that will always endure.

You have to move. You have to try. You have to experiment. You have to reach out. You have to do the thing. Action means making mistakes. One of the great things about action is that it doesn't have to be perfect. Failure of course plays a part in any great accomplishment. But the only real failure is not taking action in the first place.

Taking action can mean putting energy into a task. It can mean making a phone call, or it can mean changing the way you look at a problem. It can also mean changing your mindset, defining what makes you unique, or progressing towards the person you want to become.

Dreams are the destination
Decisions are the directions
Discipline is the difference

"You can't start a fire without a spark."

—Bruce Springsteen

7

CREATE THE SPARK

If you like to be around or on the water, Michigan is the place to be. No matter where you are standing in the "The Great Lakes State", you are never more than six miles from one of the state's 11,000 inland lakes and never more than eighty-five miles from one of the Great Lakes. Once spring finally turns to summer, the state becomes a water wonderland for residents and vacationers alike. The state is also home to several islands, with Mackinac (pronounced Mak-in-aw) as the most famous and popular.

Located in between the upper and lower peninsulas and where Lake Michigan and Lake Huron come together in the Straits of Mackinac, the island can only be reached by boat or ferry. No cars are permitted, and the only modes of transportation once you're on the island are horse-drawn carriages and bicycles. The streets are lined with Victorian-style hotels and fudge shops. Arriving there feels as if you've stepped into another world.

Perhaps the most significant feature of the island is the majestic and luxurious Grand Hotel, boasting the largest front porch in the world with over one hundred oversized rocking chairs. A favorite activity of hotel guests is to sit in one and stare out at the water or take in the awesome presence of the Mackinac Bridge, which connects the two peninsulas. During my last visit to the island with

Christina, we strolled out onto the massive porch to watch the sunset after enjoying a fantastic dinner.

As we settled into our chairs, I noticed there seemed to be an unusual amount of sailboats entering the harbor all at once. Not just a handful, but dozens and more on the way. This wasn't a coincidence; this was an event. There were onlookers gathered by the water's edge cheering and applauding. A gentleman nearby gave me the rundown on the Chicago Yacht Club's Race to Mackinac.

Every year, sailors from around the world gather to compete and test their sailing prowess in the largest annual freshwater distance race in the world. The race covers 333 miles and is an exhausting challenge of a competitor's will and the crew's ability to work together to overcome adversity. I imagined their sense of accomplishment at the conclusion of the race. A race of that magnitude and all that it entails is quite a challenge to take on and brings with it a degree of risk. Stepping onto one of those beautiful vessels is stepping into an arena fraught with variables. Fatigue and changing weather are just a couple of the issues that the sailors must endure over the course of the race.

So as I relaxed on the deck of the Grand Hotel, I imagined how much the sailors were looking forward to resting not only their bodies but their minds as well, once they finally saw the finish line. As the sun sank in the sky, the number of boats anchored in the harbor seemed to increase by the minute.

After several days of constant motion on the open water, it must have felt amazing to drop their anchors into the lake. I started to think about how the anchor, while completely unused during the race, may just be the most important part of a boat. It's out of the way when you don't need it, but it is always available when you do.

WHY DO WE NEED DREAMS?

Dreams are your anchor. They are kept on board your ship and their presence allows the fire inside you to continue to burn even in the face of rough waters. When the obstacles seem too great to overcome or when the waves crash over the deck of your boat, your dreams will direct you to the closest harbor. They will allow you to craft your vision of what your future will look and feel like.

As I mentioned in the introduction to this book, when my first dream died, I drifted. Without realizing just how important having an anchor was, my boat was slowly moving out to sea. The movement was gradual and constant. But without direction and a destination, the boat ended up in places I never intended to visit. I landed in jobs that didn't light me up, lived in a constant state of frustration, and my relationships suffered as a result. I spent hardly any time shaping a vision of what I wanted my life to look like because my dreams were wrapped up in things that were no longer available to me. I didn't know how to advance toward a new vision.

Dreams anchor you to the burning question of *Who could I become?* Establishing a vision for your life provides great clarity and prevents you from losing your way or drifting off course. Without it, and without noticing, you could end up miles from where you hoped you'd end up. That's not to say that everything will go according to this vision or that you won't have to adjust your sails along the way to account for the change in wind. But the vision brings your dreams back into focus. Your feelings of inspiration and hope will begin to kick in, and you'll start to feel motivated to follow that vision.

Why did you play sports? What called you and pushed you to show up each and every day, month after month, season after season? At the end of a long day when my muscles were tired, I was mentally drained, and I didn't think I could get up the next day and do it all over again, I did it anyway. I didn't like the pain, I didn't always love practice, and I definitely didn't enjoy the monotony of being an athlete at times. So why did I do it?

My dreams.

I had a dream for the future, for my future. I had dreams of throwing touchdown passes in the NFL. I had dreams of making my family proud of me. I had dreams of living like my heroes did. When I was a kid, I didn't dream of all the little things I had to do in order to accomplish the dream. I didn't dream of the soreness in my arm after a long practice or the burning in my chest during a conditioning session. The dream is where it all started. Dreams have to come first. The same is true for the next chapter and all the chapters that will follow in your life. Without a picture of what your future will look like, there can be no forward progress.

Dreams also give your life meaning. They fill you with hope and inject you with all the energy you need to pursue them. I believe Frankl's idea that humans make the mistake of trying to find the meaning of life as if there is one "super meaning" that needs to be discovered.

No two lives are exactly the same, so there can't be just one blanket objective for all of us to attain. Because each person is on a unique path, the meaning can even change from day to day. The more attainable objective is to find ways to make each moment meaningful. Stacking meaningful moments on top of each other creates a life that is uniquely yours.

This means you have the power to control your future. And in charting your course, you will be rewarded with the peace that comes from knowing that there's an anchor on board in moments of uncertainty. When the sky gets dark and the storm clouds roll in, there's a way to maintain an eye on the prize.

WHAT WOULD YOU STICK YOUR HAND IN THE FIRE FOR?

What do you want? What do you *really* want your life to be and to look like? Your dreams matter. They are what you live for. The hope for a better, more meaningful tomorrow is what gives meaning to today. Without a plan and a vision for the tomorrow that you want to experience in place, you run the risk of drifting out to sea.

If you don't know what your dreams are yet, you'll get there. Hopefully, by now you have at least started to think about it. If you have, know that you're in the minority. Most people drift. Most are distracted. Most make excuses or blame others. Most people also set those infamous New Year's resolutions only to give up on them a couple of weeks into the new year. Just don't be like most people.

Most avoid thinking about it

Dreams can be scary. Children are sometimes afraid to go to sleep because the anticipation of what may come in the middle of the night is frightening. The unknown is worse than the reality of what actually is. Are there monsters under the bed or in the closet? What will happen if the answer is yes?

The majority of people avoid establishing dreams for several reasons. Committing to a vision that is made up of important dreams means that there may be setbacks, risks, and discomfort along the way. It can take a lot of work to achieve the dreams. It may take a long time to get there. And what if you spend years working towards those dreams only to fall short of achieving them? What if you don't get what you want? It can hurt. It can be devastating. Sound a little too familiar?

This is the reason I wrote this book. My dream of playing professional football died and it hurt. But am I glad that I went after the dream anyway? Without a doubt. I never thought about the possibility of not realizing the dream. I never took the time; I just moved forward. I was in the dark as to what could kill the dream down the road. Had I been aware of the odds of actually reaching the dream, I don't think I would have cared.

With age, a little wisdom, and the fear of uncertainty, though, there is much more hesitation. This is especially true in such a new and unknown environment like the one athletes find themselves in after their playing days have expired. So, dreams are avoided. Or wishes are entertained and quickly brushed off as not real possibilities. Scary things get avoided.

But dreams shouldn't be scary. Dreams are the fuel that sets the fire inside of you ablaze. They light your soul on fire. They inspire and give you hope for the future—your unique future—where you have the freedom to create.

Most are overwhelmed by the thought of it

If dreams are so important, why is the enjoyable task of creating them avoided? Why don't we want to make plans and take responsibility for our futures? For many, it's because of overwhelm. When anything seems overwhelming, there is no progress. When you have too many tasks to complete, no clear idea of how to get them done, and no sense of how long it will take, the result is stagnation.

Overwhelm creates paralysis and procrastination, and it often comes from thinking too much about others' opinions. What will my family and friends think of my dreams? If you are concerned that others may judge, criticize, or otherwise try and hold you back, you won't become a big thinker. When you are focused on dreams that excite you and seem a little out of reach, they sometimes can incite feelings of jealousy and envy from those around you. Instead of letting those outside influences hold you back, keep in mind that your dreams may be instilling feelings of uneasiness in those judging you because they themselves are worried they aren't living up to their own potential.

You weren't built to play small ball. You were meant to achieve massive and significant things in this world—greater things than you've already accomplished. But those things, whatever they may be or become, start in your head. The best part is you get to choose. So if given the power to decide, why wouldn't you go for it all?

Your dreams don't have to be big, they just have to belong to you. People sometimes get scared by the idea of dreaming big because they think it has to be something that changes the world. But this isn't the case. What matters isn't the size of the dream or what someone else will think of it. All that matters is what your dreams mean to you.

THE POWER OF WHY

Sakichi Toyoda, founder of Toyoda Industries, was a Japanese inventor and industrialist who developed a very simple and effective way to solve a problem. His concept of "The 5 Whys" was created in the 1930s and became more popular and widespread in the 1970s. The technique employed by Toyoda (the company known today as Toyota) was that whenever the company encountered a problem, they wouldn't implement a solution until they drilled down on exactly what the problem was. They did this by asking "why" no less than five times. By doing this, the root cause of the problem was eventually discovered, and a solution was put in place to prevent the problem from happening again.

I have found that the concept of the "5 Whys" can also be very helpful in creating dreams. This exercise can bring awareness to your vision. It can help you decide whether the things that you want are worth pursuing and whether they will receive the necessary energy to go after them. Are they worth it? Is the reason you want them important enough to you?

You aren't meant to merely survive. You want more. You may even want it all. But achieving all your dreams isn't easy. There will be roadblocks and elements of risk that tempt you to give up or go in another direction. You won't always understand the "how" of reaching your dreams, and it will try to stop you in your tracks.

As much of a challenge as it may seem, the "how" is the easy part...once the "why" is clear and there is a belief in its importance. German philosopher Frederick Nietzsche once said, "He who has a *why* can bear almost any *how*." Knowing your *why* is a mandatory first step on the road to bringing all your important dreams to life.

DREAMS IN A BOTTLE

What sounds amazing? If you are secure enough to reveal them, dreams can be stated out loud and talked about with people that you trust. And if you are creating dreams in your mind, you are ahead of most of the general population that don't have any ambitions. They may have things that they wish for, but that's all they are—wishes. That's not what you're about. You are an action-taker. But to make your dreams a reality, you'll need to take things to the next level.

Putting your dreams on paper will sear them into your subconscious. It will also serve as a visual source of inspiration. The first step to living an epic life beyond what you've already achieved is putting pen to paper and moving those dreams out of your head. Why? Because it's been proven that if you write down your ambitions, they are 42% more likely to happen.

That's right. Just taking the critical step of writing down your dreams and visions for your future makes them more likely to take place. To be relentless in your plans for your future, you need to start by listing them. So, let's start charting your course.

The anchor list

Your written list doesn't have to be like mine or anyone else's. It just has to be yours. I like to think of mine as an "anchor list." So are you ready to build one?

Remember, an anchor's purpose is to prevent the boat from drifting. With the anchor holding the ship in place, the captain is free to work on what needs to get done. Whether that is topping off the engine's oil, mapping out the next day's course, or getting some much-needed rest, the anchor is the ultimate symbol of intention.

We all need to anchor ourselves in things that matter because inevitably, the storms will test our strength and resolve. Anchoring yourself in your dreams and ambitions will provide peace, optimism, and hope that tomorrow will be better than today.

Before we begin, I want to emphasize again that what you are about to put down on paper aren't merely wishes. Wishes don't get accomplished. They often come and go without any real desire or plan attached to them. The anchor list that you will create will be treated in your mind as if the items on it are inevitable. The question isn't *if* they will happen but *when*.

Step 1: Determine Your Deadline

A dream without a deadline is just a wish. There is much debate about how far out into the future we should look to allow our vision for our lives to become reality. Some experts ask "Where do you see yourself in ten years?" The problem with that question is that ten years is too far away. For many, trying to plan and achieve within the framework of one year can get messy. So ten years can seem like light years away. Desires change, relationships end and begin, and lessons are learned causing even the most ambitious people to have to reevaluate or abandon their dreams altogether.

We tend to overestimate what we can do in shorter time frames (like a year or a day) and underestimate what can be accomplished in longer time frames (like five or ten years.) So, I would also argue that one year is too short of a window. A year may sound like a long time, but I tend to create big dreams only to watch the time fly by because the magnitude of the dream doesn't line up with the time necessary to achieve it.

When I am having trouble determining how far out to cast the dreams I create, I pay close attention to how my energy levels respond when I read out loud the items on my list. I begin each statement with the phrase "In ____ years…" If I use a longer timeline and I feel my energy dip, I know that the distance between now and the stated deadline is too long. On the other hand, if I use a time parameter that excites me because it feels like it can be achieved in a period of time that will come relatively fast, I know it's right.

While you are free to give yourself whatever parameters you like to step into your dreams, I personally like the three-year mark. I've found that three years is just the right amount of time to allow me to achieve big things with small milestones along the way to keep me progressing. Keep in mind as well that the larger the amount of time you give yourself, the more room there is for procrastination.

Remember, this exercise doesn't merely consist of making an arbitrary list. This is what your life will look like three years from now. More importantly, it's what your life will feel like. As important as these dreams will be, what's even more significant is the type of person you will become on the way to achieving them.

Step 2: Prime Yourself

TIME AND SPACE

Big thinking requires big time and big space. Making time and space in your schedule to consider your big ideas is going to be critical to connecting with the emotions that are woven into your dream. Your mind will need time to explore. You'll need time to filter through ideas and questions. You'll need a peaceful environment to work through where you see your next three years taking shape.

These dreams and this exercise are too important to not prioritize. Put it in your calendar and start looking forward to it. In this noisy world of ours, it can be difficult to find complete silence. So find a spot on the sand at a beach or under a tree at a park. Wherever your mind feels the clearest. If silence isn't your thing and you feel more creative with a little inspiration, put some headphones on and cue up your favorite playlist.

NEVER SETTLE

In what way does selling yourself short in any way serve you? A bigger question is in what way does selling yourself short serve others? *Average, mediocre, ok, fine, just good enough.* Do any of these inspire you? Do any of these sound like you? Of course not.

Push your mind to the edge of what scares you and beyond and live there. It's more fun. Mediocre can be frustrating because, in many instances, you'd be doing the same amount of work for far less than the results you want to have in your life. Don't let those limiting beliefs creep in and shut down your big thinking. Think about what you truly want, not what you think you can have.

Don't limit yourself and don't worry about how you'll get there. Keep in mind, if you know why you want the life that you desire, you can figure out how to get it. No matter what it is, there's someone on the planet who has wanted the same thing and achieved it. So the steps to get there can be learned and followed. Why not go big? Why not go after exactly what you want? What if you become exactly who you want to be?

Step 3: Design Your Significant Sectors

The book you are reading is the first one I've written and published. It is really the first significant piece of writing that I've ever done, outside of book reports or term papers for school. So to take on such a daunting challenge, I had to learn the best way to break down the larger message that I wanted to convey to you, the reader, into groups of ideas that fit well together.

This was necessary not only for you to be able to digest everything in an easy-to-understand manner, but it was very helpful for me to categorize the themes in my own mind. *Fierce knowledge, inspired intention, relentless action,* and *epic focus* can stand on their own as different paths to victory in your life as a former athlete, but they also work together to create the overall message of creating a life that's filled with meaning and harnessing the fire within.

The same will be true for your anchor list. Your life is made up of more than one category and those sectors represent different areas of emphasis. Though not always completely separate because one can fuel another, thinking about one at a time can bring great clarity and focus to what you want to bring into your world. Think about what categories are most important to you. Keep in mind, this isn't an exercise to rush through. These dreams *will* become your reality in three years...or less.

The sectors of my life that are most important to me are *health, family, wealth, and impact.* Feel free to use these categories or come up with your own. You may choose to prioritize other areas such as *giving* or your *occupation*. Whichever way you go, own it. Once you have your sectors figured out, write down the name of the sector and create a section to write in. Next, fill in what your life will look like in three years in each of the sectors.

Below is each of my sectors and an example of what I want to achieve in that category.

- **Health**: I am in the best shape of my life, not only on the outside but on the inside as well.
- **Family**: Our family is comprised of four healthy individuals who pursue their own goals but support the dreams of the others.
- **Wealth**: Our family has a written plan that grows and evolves as our dreams do.
- **Impact**: Service to others is the core tenant of every professional venture I take on.

With your sectors identified and written down, you've already done more than most will ever do in capturing their "why". In the coming chapters, we'll build on this anchor and continue to take relentless action toward your dreams.

Stick Your Hand in the Fire

- What will anchor you when times get hard or you feel like drifting?
- Why will you do what you do?
- Are your dreams big enough to push the limits of what you think is possible for you?
- What or who would you stick your hand in the fire for?

"Hard choices, easy life. Easy choices, hard life."

—Jerzy Gregorek

8

FAN THE FLAMES

On October 16, 1962, President John F. Kennedy and his administration were shocked to learn that the Soviet Union was installing medium-range missiles on the island country of Cuba. In the middle of the Cold War, this move not only signaled an aggressive and dangerous nuclear threat from the Soviets but created a sense of urgency, given that Cuba was only 90 miles off the coast of Florida. These events brought the two countries—and the entire world—to the brink of a nuclear war that, once started, would create only losers.

Kennedy's top military advisors strongly urged the President to launch an invasion of Cuba. In their eyes, any other course of action would be a sign of weakness and would lessen the prestige of the American might in the eyes of the rest of the world. Kennedy, during a national television address on October 22, decided instead to issue a blockade. He ordered the US military to "quarantine" Cuba, preventing any more Soviet ships from delivering missiles there. The Soviet ships eventually turned around and backed down, effectively ending the standoff and allowing the world to finally exhale.

Had Kennedy listened to his own advisors, none of us might have lived to hear about thirteen of the most tense and pivotal days in modern history. Imagine the pressure of the situation and how strong the urge must have been to follow the advice of the people who are the best in the world at assessing these situations. Kennedy showed unbelievable poise and restraint but more importantly, he displayed the ability and the courage to make his own decisions.

Like the dreams you wrote down in the last chapter, JFK had a dream for the country. He had a clear vision for the nation and a strong belief that both he and Soviet leader Nikita Khrushchev wanted to avoid an unprecedented nuclear war. He saw a future America, and he never wavered from this dream—a dream that served as an anchor to guide what would've otherwise been an impossible decision to make.

DREAMS AND DECISIONS

Dreams only become meaningful when you connect them to your decisions.

The decisions that you make regarding your future won't decide the fate of the world at large, (although they could), but they will without question impact the future of *your* world. Fortunately for all of us, there is a power that we all possess that can provide us with everything we could ever hope for and much more. The power to make our own decisions. To decide our futures instead of having them determined for us. Don't make the mistake of taking this power for granted. You have the world of opportunity at your fingertips and need to understand the freedom that you have so you can best use it to your advantage.

Fuel by itself cannot start a fire, but the fuel of your dreams combined with the oxygen from your decisions can start a reaction that builds momentum and a life that's moving forward and filled with meaning. Let's look at the four decisions that you can apply to your dreams.

THE FOUR DECISIONS

You and I are constantly presented with choices, making about 35,000 decisions per day. On one hand, the power to choose can be considered the greatest and most underrated of human freedoms. On the other hand, it can certainly become a paralyzing prison of sorts, if you allow it to be.

Every day you are tested and tempted by the options you have available to you, and the choices you make shape your day and ultimately your future. Decisions can include whether to get out of bed when the alarm goes off or hit the snooze button, whether to eat Lucky Charms or oatmeal for breakfast, what shirt to wear, whether to work out or not, and what route to take to work. And these are just a portion of the choices that need to be made prior to 8 a.m. Extra shot of espresso? You might consider saying yes to this one so you have the energy needed to make all the other decisions that will come your way before your head hits the pillow that night.

Does all that decision-making sound tiring to you? If so, it just might be contributing to a phenomenon known as *decision fatigue*. While research has yet to come up with definitive ways to say with certainty that it is actually based in fact, decision fatigue is worth assessing in your situation. If nothing else, doesn't it make sense to shine a light on your decisions to see whether they are helping you or hurting you?

More to the point, are the daily decisions you make aligned with your dreams? After all, you made the crucial decision to take the time to spend precious mental energy on thinking about your vision for your life in the next three years on paper. That was a big step towards defining who you will become in the future.

Imagine decision fatigue as the battery indicator on your cell phone. You start your day with a full charge because you got a good night's sleep. But as the day goes on and you are faced with an increasing amount of decisions to make, your battery starts to slowly drain. Too many choices will lead to you needing another charge.

But how many of us stop and ask ourselves if the decisions we are making are pulling us in the direction we want to go or pulling us away from what matters most? And where do we start? First, let's acknowledge that some decisions need to be made whether we want to make them or not. Let's also understand that some decisions carry more weight than others. Whether your shoes match the rest of your outfit is less significant than whether you choose to stop working out on a regular basis so you can free up time to eat gallons of mint chocolate chip ice cream and humongous plates of nachos. The overwhelming sea of choices demands that we have a system in place so we don't get lost in the waves of our choices.

A simple yet effective way to be certain that there is a path from our dreams to our decisions is to understand the only meaningful decisions that matter. That's not to say that you have to spend your entire day only moving toward your dreams. There should always be a little space for other things that are a bit more frivolous than what the future holds.

If you're feeling bogged down with the sheer number of choices that need to be made, though, or if you find yourself not taking enough action on the right things because you're not sure what you should be working on, there's a way to distill everything down and categorize those thousands of decisions into just four: the controllable, the uncontrollable, the non-negotiable, the unacceptable.

The controllable

Michael Phelps is the most decorated Olympic athlete in history. His 28 total and 23 gold medals are more than any other athlete has ever achieved. Over the course of his career, he dominated various swimming events, including the 400-meter individual medley, the 200-meter individual medley, and the 200-meter freestyle.

Since retiring in 2016, Phelps has kept himself busy with various issues relating to mental health and overall fitness. So when the 2020 Olympics were postponed due to the worldwide COVID-19 pandemic, he naturally was asked by major media outlets what advice he would offer to those Olympic athletes whose dreams of competing in the games were put on pause while waiting for the 2021 games in Tokyo, Japan.

His advice? Concentrate on what you can control. Amid so many unprecedented unknowns, this is outstanding and timely advice. But it's not reserved solely for athletes who are dealing with a shutdown never seen in our lifetime. It can be used by anyone at any time. The athletes in limbo could control their training regime, what they ate, how much sleep they prioritized, and a long list of other variables.

There's no doubt that you've heard this advice more than once during your playing career. (Advice that actually works usually tends to get repeated.) Knowing the theory and actually implementing it, though, are two different things. Easier said than done.

The same is true now for you as you advance to the next phase of your life. Now that there are no longer competitive events to train for, let's identify and exercise the things that you can take control of, not just daily, but moment by moment. There are only two things that you can always control.

Attitude

Your greatest freedom is not the ability to choose who your friends are, or what city to live in. It's not even the freedom to choose how to spend your day or what to watch on YouTube. It's the freedom to choose your attitude. You have the privilege of being able to frame any situation, including the most tragic and seemingly dire, into one of meaning and significance.

Most people believe, either consciously or subconsciously, that their attitude, or mood, is a result of their circumstances. If someone cuts you off in traffic, does it affect your conversation with the next person you talk to? If your day starts off on the wrong foot, does it cause the rest of the day to go downhill? Most people don't realize the control that they have in any given set of circumstances.

Do you have the one person in your life who seems to be upbeat and smiling through every circumstance, regardless of whether it's negative or positive? No matter what, they are the same every day in every way. It's not that they don't have bad days or get frustrated with certain people. How they were raised or what's in their DNA may contribute to their overall disposition. But those people make different choices about their attitude. And those choices become who they are.

Your attitude is made up of three essential elements: thoughts, feelings, and actions. Your thoughts are what your conscious mind thinks about a situation. They, in turn, influence how you feel about that situation. And your feelings affect your actions.

Effort

The late Kobe Bryant's name was and always will be synonymous with a crazy work ethic. The stories are legendary. From his former Lakers coach Byron Scott finding Bryant shooting in a dark gym two hours before practice to refusing to leave the gym until he made 800 shots. His effort was unmatched by even the other great players in the NBA. He even played left-handed during a game because of an injury to his right shoulder.

No one in the sport gave greater effort and devotion to his dream of becoming a champion. He could control getting out of bed and heading to the gym before everyone else. He could control how much extra work he chose to invest in. And he made the decision to take full advantage of those freedoms. Even when other professional athletes were asleep, Bryant was grinding away at his craft. Those colleagues had similar aspirations. They dreamt of being champions too. They just chose to make different decisions.

The uncontrollable

To try to control what you can't is wasteful. Your energy will get depleted and will be wasted on a fruitless attempt to satisfy your own expectations. That precious energy could've been directed toward your bigger dreams.

You will find that, now that you've stepped outside the arena, there are far more things that you can't control than those that you can. The lack of control will be uncomfortable at times. That's good. It will serve as a sign that you need to concentrate on those things that you can affect. The uncontrollable things that will inevitably try to test you on a regular basis are meant to keep you from your dreams. They are there to slow you down and distract you. Don't let that happen. You have too much to do. These uncontrollables are mental traps.

How do you avoid the trap?

1. Recognize that what you are focused on now is uncontrollable
2. Quickly return your attention back to something you can control

Conditions

Victory is based on internal decisions, not external conditions. In outdoor sports, weather can be a huge factor. Wind, rain, snow, the conditions of the playing surface. These all can come into play and affect the results of the game. But you can't control them. You can't cancel the game because the conditions aren't ideal.

In a 1988 NFL playoff game between the Philadelphia Eagles and the Chicago Bears, a heavy and dense fog rolled into Chicago's Soldier Field and settled right above the turf. Unable to see more than a few yards down the field, the team's offenses were forced to mostly run the ball instead of throwing it. Waiting for the fog to clear or deciding to play the game on a different day simply weren't options. Thousands of fans showed up to be entertained. The game had to be played. So decisions had to be made regardless of the conditions. What were the strategies to work around the uncontrollable weather? Could it be used as an advantage?

Conditions will change in your world, often without warning. Tides will turn. Winds of change will sweep through at high speeds. So what do you do? Embrace the conditions and decide to handle them confidently regardless of what they are. Go inside yourself and revert to the freedom that is always at your disposal. Decide to weather the storm no matter where it comes from.

Other People

As hard as you may try, you can't control other people. Other people are often where we look to get affirmation for what we are, what we believe, and the things we want. But people aren't always going to deliver on what you want from them. They are going to disagree with what you are becoming and doubt your chances of success. They are on their own path and that will often be a different one than you're on. You can't control what they do. If you're the only one who can control your actions and decisions, doesn't the same hold true for others?

Contrary to what many believe, you can't control what others think, especially of you. People have their own biases and personal interests that they want to protect. Changing someone to fit into the mold of what you want them to be is a battle that can't be won. So get laser-focused on who you are becoming and where you are headed. There is only one person in the world you can control—you. So get started today. Get better today by making the decision to not waste time and energy on other people.

But what about investing in relationships? Of course, that's a worthwhile pursuit. It is one of life's greatest providers of meaning and purpose. But just know that relationships, unlike sports, are not competitions. They can't be won. Enjoy them and learn from them.

I've found that the best way to resist the urge of trying to control what others do, say, and think is to have zero expectations for them. When you lower your expectations for things that are out of your control, you are rarely disappointed. Have high expectations for yourself, no expectations of others.

The Outcome

You can control the inputs; you can't control the outcomes. In every situation, there are variables that will factor into the outcome that are beyond your control. Sometimes, you've done everything right, but the other team is just a little bit better. A little bit more talented. The ball bounces their way and not yours. The scoreboard doesn't reflect how hard you worked to put yourself in a position to be victorious. It won't seem fair, and it won't make sense. All you can control is everything that leads up to the actual final score.

Who won? What was the final score? These are the questions that get asked after a game. No one ever asks questions like "Who gave everything they had?" "Who put in the extra time to prepare when no one was looking?" Detach from the outcome. Resist the urge to look at the results. You will have to be the only one asking yourself whether you can let go of the outcome because you decided to do the work.

The Past

Sharks don't swim backward. The bodies of sharks are designed to allow them to move through the water quickly. But when sharks attempt to move backward, the shape of their fins doesn't allow it. The bigger reason that these ocean predators don't swim in reverse is that doing so would lead to their death. Their bodies are shaped in such a way that swimming forward allows the water to run over their gills. Moving backwards would force the water into their gills causing them to drown. They are always looking ahead. Moving forward.

What's behind you is important, and it's a part of who you are. But you can't control it. You can't go back and change it. What's done is done. The decisions of the past can't be undone. That doesn't mean that there isn't value in your history. You can learn from it, carry it with you, and refer to it when doing so can provide a lesson on how to handle the not-so-pleasant present. It can be a good indicator of future decisions or a reason to course-correct. It can fan the flames of your ambition. But it's out of your control. Dwelling on the past only keeps you from stepping into your future. As Frankl suggests, "When we are no longer able to change a situation, we are challenged to change ourselves."

In short, you can't control things that you'd like to control—conditions, other people, outcomes, and your past. Attempting to do so manifests itself inside your body and your mind as stress. The resulting stress takes a toll on your body because stress hormones are released when frustration takes hold of you. The stress takes an equally large chunk of your mental energy reserves. And all of it robs you of the possibility of moving closer to your dreams but controlling what you can control. Decide to let go of what you can't control and get yourself dialed in on what you can.

The non-negotiable

To bridge the gap between where you stand at this moment and reaching the dreams that you've put into place, you will have to take a stand. Planting your flag is required. There is a need for the creation of concrete personal boundaries and rules. Non-negotiables leave no room for debate. When you have a non-negotiable in place, you can't be talked out of it under any circumstances. These personal standards require an unwavering commitment on your part.

What are your standards? The more invested and emotionally attached you are to the dream, the easier it is to make the commitment to that which can't be altered because of an outside force. The door can't remain cracked open to allow the possibility of letting others knock you off track or dip below your standards. And make no mistake, they will try.

Want to reduce stress and be happier? Decide. Decide what you will do and what you won't. Decide to be unflappable in your dedication to your standards. This is not the easy path. Your resolve will be tested by those who don't have standards that mean something to them.

Do you already have standards but feel as though they are too low to achieve the life you want to have and the person you want to be? Raise them. Jack them up to a ridiculous level and hold yourself to them. Does that sound difficult? That's because it is.

Setting a high standard requires leadership and courage. But you've decided what you envision for the future, now decide what daily steps must be taken in order to pull those dreams closer to you.

And non-negotiables are much more powerful when they are acted upon every single day. One small decision at a time clarifies the path to living the life you've imagined.

Top 5 Benefits Of Non-Negotiables

1. Higher chance of accomplishing your dreams and living the life you dream about
2. Shapes your identity and the person you are becoming
3. Simplifies decisions
4. Increases self-respect and respect from others
5. Impacts your overall mental and physical health

The Power Of "I Will"

Words matter. And who says the words matters just as much as the words themselves. The words you use both in your head and aloud will have an impact on your ultimate success. When establishing your non-negotiables, your words can provide the oxygen that gives life to your personal standards.

Take a hard-line approach with yourself and your ambitions. They matter, and how you talk about them and think about them matters too. Words like *if*, *maybe*, and *try* aren't going to cut it. Write down your daily non-negotiables and preface them all with these two words: "I will..."

Here are two of my non-negotiables:

1. *I will lift weights for 60 minutes 3 times a week.*
2. *I will wake at 5:45 every day (even weekends) to allow myself to mentally prepare for the day.*

What will your non-negotiables be? Take a moment to think about them and write them down. Write them out every day if that's what it takes to solidify them in your mind. Turn them into a poster and hang them on your wall. Say them out loud. Repeat. Pay attention to how you feel when you start each sentence with "I will."

The unacceptable

As athletes and as humans, we all have certain beliefs, values, and preferences that make us unique. These differences in opinions, choices, and lifestyles make us diverse and help us grow as individuals. However, not everything that comes our way or surrounds us is acceptable and that is why it is important to determine what is unacceptable in your life and set boundaries accordingly.

Unacceptable things can vary from person to person. For instance, some people may find smoking and drinking to be unacceptable, while others may not. Similarly, some people may prioritize their physical and mental health over their career while others may not. Therefore, it is crucial to identify your values and principles to decide what is unacceptable in your life. There are a few ways to figure out what is unacceptable in your life.

Reflect on your past experiences

Reflecting on your past experiences and considering what made you unhappy or uncomfortable is a good starting point. For instance, if you had a toxic relationship or an unhealthy work environment, take note of what you didn't like and make sure to avoid such situations in the future.

Identify your values

Our values are the principles that guide our decision-making and shape our personalities. Identifying these values can help you understand what is important to you and what you cannot compromise on. For example, if honesty is your core value you may not tolerate dishonesty in your personal or professional relationships.

Consider your goals

Your goals and aspirations dictate the direction you want your life to take. For example, if your goal is to lead a healthy lifestyle you may not tolerate unhealthy habits such as overeating or substance abuse. Once you have determined what is unacceptable in your life, the next step is setting boundaries to communicate your values and expectations to others.

Boundaries are the limits you set for yourself that will help you maintain healthy relationships, prioritize your needs and values, and protect your mental and emotional well-being. Setting boundaries can be challenging, especially if you're used to people-pleasing or having difficulty saying no. However, it is essential to uphold these boundaries to avoid compromising on what you deem unacceptable.

Some ways to set boundaries include:

1. Communicate your boundaries clearly. Be assertive and communicate your boundaries in a clear and respectful manner. For example, if you do not want to work overtime let your boss know in advance and explain why.
2. Stick to your boundaries. It is crucial to stick to your boundaries even if others do not respect or understand them. For instance, if you've decided to cut off toxic people from your life, do so without feeling guilty.
3. Be open to negotiation. It is important to be flexible and open in negotiation when setting boundaries. For example, you can negotiate a compromise if your partner wants to spend time with friends, but you also want to have private time together.

Determining what is unacceptable in one's life and setting boundaries are crucial steps toward maintaining healthy relationships, promoting personal growth, and leading a fulfilling and meaningful life. It requires introspection, self-awareness, and assertiveness, but it is worth the effort to create a life that aligns with your values and aspirations.

Many of us follow certain paths simply because they present themselves. Often, however, these paths lead in directions or take you places you really don't want to be. You can save yourself enormous amounts of time and energy by asking the simple, straightforward question, "Where is this decision likely to lead?" Then pay close attention to the answer.

Stick Your Hand in the Fire

- Where will you decide to place your energy?
- What actions and thoughts can you control?
- What is out of your control?
- What will you choose to make non-negotiable in your life?
- What will you choose to not accept in your life?

"Discipline equals freedom."

—Jocko Willink

9

FEEL THE HEAT

In ancient Greece, about 2500 years ago, a group of warriors known as Spartans reigned supreme. They were so relentless and fierce that they were depicted and immortalized in the 2006 film *300* as fearless and dedicated fighters. The Spartans arose from the city-state of Sparta in ancient Greece. Their central belief was that they existed to fight. Their purpose in life was war. And the Spartans did not dabble.

Every Spartan male was molded from birth with the vision that one day he too would fight in battle. Starting at the age of seven, a boy would begin his training for battle. He was conditioned to overcome his fears and strengthen his body. He was taught from a young age that he should "come home with his shield or be carried on it."

The most famous Spartan battle ultimately ended in defeat for these super soldiers. During the battle of Thermopylae, the Spartans were determined to stop the advancement of the Persians as they attempted to pass through a narrow section of the region. Clearly outnumbered 100,000 to 300, the Spartans believed that there was no greater honor than to die in battle. Rather than retreat, they decided to stand and fight. After heroically standing their ground and defending their land for two straight days, the Spartans were betrayed by a fighter who told the Persian army of an alternative way around the Spartan defense.

The Spartans have been admired and emulated for centuries because of the many stoic elements of their overall philosophy, including minimalism, disdain for luxury, brevity of speech, and attention to their overall physical health. But one practice was a prerequisite for all the other virtues that embodied a Spartan. Discipline.

What does it take to stick to the decisions that you made? Discipline. Not just the run-of-the-mill kind nor the kind from any outside force. Instead, it takes self-discipline. As an athlete, much of your discipline most likely came from the external pressures of deadlines, expectations from others, and coaches pushing you to and past your limitations. But they weren't in your bedroom when the alarm clock went off at 5:30 a.m.

Self-discipline is the highest form of self-respect. Now that your time in the arena has ended, those external conditions that tell you where to be, when to be there, and who to be are gone. Discipline is what drives all your decisions. And your decisions get you closer to your dreams.

No one and no thing can give you the discipline you'll need outside the arena. You'll need to fight harder than ever to create it for yourself. Discipline comes from inside of you, and nowhere else. If there are other factors that bring discipline into your world, don't count on them to always be there. They may be fleeting, lose their power over time, or not be as invested in your dreams as you are. It needs to come from a place deep within your soul.

You have everything you need to build a fortress of self-discipline, by cultivating the key elements of **sacrifice, willpower**, and **habits**. Through these attitudes and practices, you can experience the freedom that comes as the result of self-discipline. In the absence of these critical practices, though, you could quite possibly destroy yourself.

SACRIFICE

Words like suffering and sacrifice and willpower and even discipline probably stir up feelings of punishment. What if instead, you looked at those ideas as opportunities? We know instinctively that most good things come our way because of hard work and a willingness to be uncomfortable. The things we want—that we are truly passionate about—are paid for with sacrifice.

Passio Bellator

Passion. This one word evokes warm and fuzzy feelings about something that you love to do. One seven-letter word brings to mind something that switches on a light inside of you. What comes to mind when you hear the word passion? Is it working with kids? Is it triathlons? Art?

When people have had great success in doing something they are passionate about, the tendency of those looking on is to think that they had superior talent and natural innate abilities that brought them rare success. After all, that's one of the reasons that fans flock to watch athletes compete. We are all attracted to people who possess impressive talents that most others don't have.

I'm impressed by expert guitar players and entrepreneurs who have built empires from the ground up. I marvel at how easy it looks for Jimi Hendrix to solo for five solid minutes without looking at the fretboard. I shake my head at how the Nike swoosh seems to be everywhere and the impact that it's had on millions around the globe. To become an icon that we all are in awe of, the mission had to be driven by an unreal level of passion.

Passion is derived from the Latin phrase *passio bellator*, which means "suffering warrior." What isn't usually thought of when you hear the word passion is the other side to the story—the sacrifice it took to accomplish the result that everyone sees. With the push of a button on the remote control, fans tune in to see a triumph on center court. There is no camera rolling on the early morning workout sessions or the late-night solo learning sessions. There's just you. With only your passion to keep you company. I'm not suggesting that suffering unnecessarily is a way to accomplish your dreams, but dreams worth living will come with a price.

Maria Mania

Maria Sharapova rose through the tennis ranks to become the number one player in the world at the height of her success. She was a five-time Grand Slam winner, upsetting the legendary Serena Williams for her first Wimbledon title in 2004. But it would've never happened, and the world would not know her name, if not for great sacrifice.

When she was six, her father made it his life's mission to cultivate the obvious talent that his daughter possessed. Yuri Sharapova was not happy with the family's circumstances in their homeland of Russia. The area of the country where they were from, Gomel, was unstable and it was difficult to make a living. And if that wasn't enough to make the family consider what they wanted their futures to look like, a nuclear accident at the Chernobyl plant had many Russian families fleeing the area.

So when Maria's father heard of a showcase for young tennis players in Moscow, he quickly made sure that Maria was there to show off her talents. While she was one of the youngest players there, she still stood out. It was becoming increasingly clear that if

Maria was to reach her full potential, she would have to take her skills to the United States.

It was not as easy to hop on a plane and fly from one country to another as you might think, however. Maria's dad had to secure a meeting with a government official and convince him that Maria was a child prodigy. Amazingly, the official relented and the visas were granted. But there was a problem. They were given only two. Maria's mother would have to remain in Russia.

Once they arrived in Miami, they didn't quite know what to do. Maria's father had $700 rolled up in his front pocket so it wouldn't be stolen. Neither one of them spoke more than a couple words of English. Now here they were in a foreign country without any friends, without any family other than each other, and they weren't even sure what to do next.

During the plane ride, Maria's father befriended a Russian couple who became fascinated, and to an extent, invested in Maria and her dad's quest for a better life in America.

They helped Yuri and Maria in several ways. It was Sunday night when they arrived, and nothing was open. There were no cell phones, no hotels available, and no one to turn to for help. Just imagine arriving in a foreign country in the middle of the night, you don't speak the language and you have no plan. Just a dream. But the Russian couple was eager to help. They had already booked a hotel room and we're more familiar with the customs in the United States. So they offered to allow Maria and her father to sleep on their hotel floor and to get themselves together while they figured out the next step.

The next morning, Yuri started making several phone calls to local tennis academies. The second one he tried was the Nick Bollettieri Tennis Academy in Bradenton, Florida. Bollettieri had a reputation for grooming major tennis stars like Andre Agassi, Jim Courier, and Anna Kournikova at his prestigious facility. Young Maria was given a tryout of sorts with an instructor. After just a few minutes of hitting with the young phenom, the instructor found a phone and called Bollettieri. Immediately the veteran talent evaluator recognized something special in Maria.

Her skill level was obvious but still needed improvement. And at six years old, she still had a lot of development ahead of her. But the one thing that set her apart was her discipline. The ability to hit balls for long periods of time without losing concentration was her competitive edge. The comfort she had with the mundane and the routine is something that even the most physically gifted players struggle with, especially at such a young age. The discipline to do something over and over again without getting bored was what Bollettieri noticed as one attribute that all champions shared.

Although she was still too young to attend the academy, an arrangement was worked out that allowed her to train there and eat there as well. As for her father, he was given a place to stay and meals as well. Maria would not see her mother again until almost three years later. Maria Sharapova and her father made sacrifices that most of us wouldn't be courageous enough to act upon.

Your dreams may not require that you move to a foreign country without your family. But they will require sacrifice.

Delayed gratification

One way to create abundance in your life is to actually embrace scarcity. Here's what I mean. As we have discussed, abundance is the belief that there is enough of everything. Enough food, enough money, and enough prosperity for everyone including you. Scarcity is the opposite. It's the idea that there is only so much pie to slice for everyone, so the bigger someone else's piece, the smaller yours must be.

To intentionally create scarcity for yourself on a micro level has tremendous benefits for you. In an age when you can get anything you want and fulfill any want at any time of day, why in the world would you choose to *not* do it? Why would you want to intentionally deprive yourself of pleasure that's so easy to attain? Because you're willing to be different. Because you've decided to be extraordinary, and you've decided to push yourself past your limits to grab what belongs to you.

Over a half century ago in the 1960's, a professor at Stanford University by the name of Walter Mischel decided to test the merits of delayed gratification. He enlisted the help of hundreds of children as his test subjects as he conducted what is now the most famous and enduring proof that delayed gratification can benefit you in almost every area of your life.

Known as the "Marshmallow Experiment," children were each placed in a private room and presented with a marshmallow. The researcher then informed the child that he had to leave the room, and if the child could restrain himself from eating the sweet treat, they would receive a second marshmallow. But if the child succumbed to the temptation and ate the treat, they wouldn't receive the second one. The results were interesting, to say the least. Some of the kids gave in and ate the treat right away. Others were able to show some temporary self-restraint but eventually ate it anyway. The smallest number of children were those who were able to hang on long enough to get both marshmallows. But that's not even the most fascinating part of the experiment.

The researchers decided to commit to tracking the children through the next forty years of their lives. What they found was that the kids who were able to delay gratification scored higher on the SATs, were better at handling stress, had a lower likelihood of obesity, and had generally better life outcomes. The longer you have to wait for something you really want, the sweeter the payoff is when you get it.

You want your dreams now. I understand that feeling. And if you don't achieve them soon enough, the temptation will be to take your foot off the gas and relax. Because of the lack of an immediate result, you may lose sight of the long-term outcomes that you're looking for. So the daily disciplines start to slip. Once becomes twice and then a year has gone by and there's been no forward movement. Zero. Delay the gratification, not the discipline.

WILLPOWER

4th Quarter Program

Willpower is underrated. My least favorite part of my college athletic experience was called the "4th Quarter Program." It was an offseason conditioning program that was as physically intense as anything I've ever done. It began in February as a lead-up to spring practice, was conducted in the dead of winter, and began every day promptly at 5:30 in the morning. For a college student, athlete or not, that was a ridiculous time to be awake. I can remember driving to the building every morning in the darkness without another car on the road at that early hour.

The only other human movement at that time was the ROTC students jogging through town. They were military students preparing for a potential battle at some point in the future; we were just football players. Why were we conditioning so intensely when there was no impending battle or game on the horizon? The season was over seven months away. Any endurance we built up over the length of the program would be lost shortly after and not benefit us in the fall. At least not physically.

These were questions that I struggled with as I conducted a mental question-and-answer session with myself during the drive to the facility. None of the analysis mattered because there was no way I was getting out of doing the hard thing that I didn't want to do at an hour that I didn't want to be awake.

The session began with a warmup that included things like wall runs, leg swings, and other exercises that left me feeling like I had been through the actual workout and not just a light warmup. Cardiovascular endurance was not a strength of mine. If the coaching staff felt like our intensity was lacking, a whistle would blow, and we'd have to start the entire session over again. Garbage cans were strategically placed around the field in case someone's stomach couldn't handle the intensity. Luckily, I never had to use one. After 90 minutes of movement with only seconds of rest in between reps, the misery would finally come to an end.

With the sun now starting to rise, I'd walk to where my car was parked. After putting the key in the ignition one particular morning, I realized something: I felt fantastic. Aside from the physical benefits, I felt mentally strong. I felt unstoppable. I took a look around and saw very little movement on campus. Everyone was still asleep. I felt hopeful and motivated to tackle the rest of the day because of the way my day had begun. On some of those days, I felt so energized that I would even remain at the building and lift weights for another hour if I didn't have class.

Head and the heart

I may have felt unstoppable when those workouts were over, but during the grueling sessions, it was a different story. There was never one moment where I enjoyed it. Every second of the workout consisted of an internal battle between what I felt like doing and what I knew I needed to do to keep my dream alive. My head was at war with my heart. My brain was arguing with my emotions. And I didn't want to be a part of it. I would've been happy to take a seat on the bench and let them hash it out without me. But I didn't have that option. Instead, I had to witness the carnage that was piling up inside of me as the whistles blew and the muscle fibers burned. I just wanted to stop moving. Who would win out, reason or emotion? My head or my heart? I was too tired and breathless to even decide who I was rooting for.

I didn't realize it at the time, but I've come to understand that these two factions of willpower actually work together and not against each other. When emotions like fear, anger, or frustration scream that it's time to stop, my head would list all the reasons why that simply wasn't a good idea. The logic in my brain urged my tired body to keep going because stopping would be letting myself down. Quitting would mean letting my teammates down. It would be a vote for myself and a vote against my team. No can do. That wasn't going to happen.

When my brain was making a great case full of excuses and rationalizations as to why it would be okay to pull up and take a few reps off, my emotions picked up the slack. My mind would tell my body stories of why it was a good idea to take it easy. No need to risk pulling a hamstring or turning an ankle. (My brain somehow forgot that any meaningful games were still months away.) That's when the emotional reserves would kick and take control. Fear, desire, and anger are powerful drivers when called upon in extreme circumstances. And these were the most demanding of circumstances. Nonstop movement with very little or no rest in between. My emotions took over when my brain was out to lunch. Both emotion and reason were only so talented on their own. But they made a great team when they worked together.

HABITS

Success isn't an event, it's a process. You know this better than anyone. The long days at the track working on your explosion out of the blocks. The late nights at the batting cage by yourself. The hours and hours of shooting free throws. The fans show up at the arena to see the finished product. They turn on the TV to see the results. What they are really looking at and what the athletes are really celebrating is the culmination of thousands of repetitions and minutes, hours, days, and years of tiny little habits performed over and over. Sometimes these are accomplished inches at a time. Steadily, those small movements began to stack on top of each other. Eventually, they lead to some big results.

Compound interest

Compound interest is a concept often used in finance to describe the growth of a sum of money over time. It's the interest earned on the principle of an investment, as well as on any accumulated interest. However, compound interest can also be applied to personal goals and success in life, as it helps you want to achieve your dreams by growing small investments over time.

The concept of compound interest isn't unlike the process of creating your dreams and success in life. Just like the growth of investments, the process of personal growth and success is a gradual one that requires consistent effort and investment over time. In this context, compound interest can be seen as a way to harness the power of time and effort to achieve one's goals and dreams.

For example, let's say you want to start a business. To achieve your dream, you need to invest time, effort, and capital into the business. Initially, returns on your investment may be low or nonexistent. However, as you continue to invest in your venture, returns will grow over time, just like compound interest on investment. The key to achieving success through compound interest is to start small and be consistent. Just like a small investment can grow into a significant amount over time, small daily habits can compound and lead to significant changes over time.

You couldn't do fifty pushups the first time you attempted the movement. You most likely started with one or two and gradually built up from there. This approach can include habits such as reading daily, working out, or meditating. By consistently investing in these habits, you can grow your knowledge, health, and mental well-being over time in the same way you were able to run faster, jump higher, or throw farther. As you should already know, failures do not define your success or limit your potential.

Finally, the principle of compound interest can also be applied to relationships and social networks. As you invest time and effort into these, you create more opportunities for success. By understanding the power of small investments consistently after overtime, individuals can harness the power of time and effort to achieve their goals.

Start small. Be consistent. Focus on the long term.

Stick Your Hand in the Fire

- What's the smallest sacrifice you made that's led to a big payoff?
- Can you make yourself do the hard thing even when you don't feel like it?
- What's one habit you'd like to create? Why?
- What's one habit you'd like to eliminate? Why?

E

Part Four

EPIC FOCUS

Storms generally move from West to East in the United States. If you've ever looked at the radar on a weather app, you've seen the various colors representing the rain and snow approaching your city. Whether you're worried about the storms altering your travel plans or affecting your ability to go for a long run, the answers to your current and future weather concerns are just a few clicks away. The app not only shows you where the storms are coming from but when they'll be arriving and how long they'll stick around. And if that wasn't enough, you're advised on exactly what you can do to best get through the storm as safely as possible.

    The rest of the animal planet doesn't have smartphones in their pockets. Colorado is one of the few places where both buffalo and cows exist, roaming the state because of two very different landscapes within its borders. One half of the state is mountainous, occupied by the great Rocky Mountains. The other half of the state is more like states to the east because of its flat topography.

Neither buffalo nor cows need technology to know when a storm is coming. They can both sense it. More interesting though is how buffalo and cows react so differently when a storm is approaching. Cows feel the storm coming from the west and start moving east, the same direction that the storm is moving. Because of this (and the fact that cows aren't the fastest animals roaming the countryside), they stay in the storm longer, never able to outrun it. That means they endure the wind, rain, snow, and discomfort that comes along with the elements for a longer period of time.

Buffalo, on the other hand, chooses to focus on the problem in a much different way. Instead of moving with the storm, they will run directly into it, not away from it. As a result, they are in the storm for a shorter amount of time. They focus on attacking the storm rather than trying to avoid it.

If you are deeply committed to using your athletic experiences and your innate talents to have a greater impact outside the arena than you did on the inside and continue to be the hero of your story, you'll need a *heroic focus*. You'll need an extraordinary amount of dialed-in, laser-like perspective on what's most important to you.

Remember what fueled the meaning that athletics gave you? Your commitment to the arena was uncommon and courageous. Your effort and consistency were unusual. Your dedication seemed routine and common to you but in the larger scope, it was epic.

Heroes see what others can't. They look for things that aren't easily seen by everyone. They are willing to do the hard and unusual things that aren't obvious. Heroes are exceptional, not just in their results and their accomplishments, but in the road they took to get those results. In the quiet time, before the sun comes up and after it goes down, they simply move forward.

Where will you focus your attention when the storm rolls in? In which direction will you move when adversity comes over the ridge? What will inspire your urge to move in one direction versus the other? The desire to avoid pain, uncertainty, and work...or the ambition to live a life that changes your own and the lives of others? The appetite to minimize future regrets...or the craving to feel comfortable now?

It's time to head bravely into the storm.

"The gem cannot be polished without friction, nor man perfected without trials."

—Confucius

10

NO FRICTION, NO FIRE

The Grand Canyon is one of the most popular hiking spots in the U.S. and probably on the bucket list of most adventurers. Hailed as one of the most breathtaking places on the planet, the Arizona landmark—at a length of over 270 miles—gives millions of annual visitors pause with its massive rock formations and views that command your full attention. How can one not feel insignificant standing in the shadow of something so magnificent? Because of all the twists and turns and the sheer expansiveness of the canyon, it takes about five hours to drive 220 miles from the South Rim to the North Rim, just to cover the 18-mile width of the canyon.

Hikers hoping to get more up close and personal with the beauty of the Grand Canyon embark on a trek that tests their physical stamina along with their mental fortitude. Out of more than five million visitors that make the trip to Arizona every year to see the gorge, less than one percent actually decide to step below the rim. They are the ones who take the steps necessary to challenge themselves and experience the rewards that come with those tests.

One of the most popular and most challenging hikes is one that takes you "rim to rim." The hike covers about 24 miles but takes on average two days to complete. For those who are experienced and in great shape, the trip can be covered in one day. Starting at the

North Rim, the North Kaibab Trail sends adventurers on a descent of over 14 miles and a loss of 5761 feet in elevation to the bottom of the canyon where you meet the creator of this beautiful chasm: the Colorado River. At this point, the trek is only about half over. Hikers then make the climb back up the rock ascending 4380 feet

While the destination on the other side is often visible and feels within reach, parts of the path to get there are hidden and treacherous. The steps to reach the other side are not linear and are rocky at best. The hike definitely requires some mental focus, a willingness to overcome challenges, and consistency in taking one step after another.

In the previous chapters, you painted the picture of what your life will look like three years from now. As you make important decisions and put daily disciplines into motion, you will probably feel a sensation of instability. When you first experience it, it's easy to believe that it comes from a place of inferiority. That it somehow means that something is wrong with you. It's an intense sense of frustration that you've fallen behind the pack and need to catch up. It's a tension that comes from deep within you.

But don't be fooled by what the feeling *means*. The significance of this feeling can't be overstated or emphasized enough. Make no mistake about it, this tension is the catalyst you're in search of. It's a good thing, maybe the best of things. The restlessness that you feel lying in bed at night? That signifies that there's more for you to discover and conquer. When someone is talking to you but you don't hear a word they're saying? Your mind is working on what your next step is. When your leg is bouncing under the table during dinner, know that your engines are revving up.

Embrace the tension you are currently feeling. Let yourself smile for a second and enjoy the reminder that your fire was never fully extinguished. It just has to be reignited. For your fire to turn into one that blazes, though, there needs to be friction to generate enough heat for yours to explode. No friction, no fire.

CLOSING THE GAP

That burning sensation that you feel is the friction between what you have already accomplished in the past and what you still have left to achieve in the future. Victor Frankl called it Noö Dynamics. I like to think of it as setting off on that long hike across the Grand Canyon, where the terrain changes every minute and your senses require you to be on alert, aware of what's going on around you at all times. You don't quite know what or who you will encounter, and it can be tough to distinguish between the excitement and anxiety you feel about what's in store for you.

The gap between your past achievements and what you still have yet to conquer in your life can feel as long and as wide as the Grand Canyon. In fact, sometimes it can feel like there is no way to get from one side to the other or know which path to take, let alone where to start. If you started the trek off without any knowledge of how to refuel your energy reserves, you wouldn't make it.

The hike from where you stand now and the destination on the other side will be cloudy at times. There will be uneven terrain and moments where you walk along the edge of a cliff without anything to hold onto. There will be high moments like watching the sunrise on the horizon or celebrating your wedding day. There will be low points such as pain in your knees or the loss of a loved one. But the point of the trip is of course the trip itself. It is the experience, not just getting to the other side. And more importantly, the meaning that you attach to every step of the journey.

The following three mindsets will demand that you focus on bridging the gap between where you are now and where you want to go. They will begin to connect the tough decisions that you made in the past, the discipline you committed to for the present, and the dreams for your future that you've likely written down. These concepts will help push aside all that doesn't matter today...or won't when it's all said and done. Finally, these three elements will force you to zero in on who you want to become and the urgency that it will take to assist you in achieving all that you're capable of.

NO REGRETS?

"No regrets". This statement always gives me pause. When I hear a celebrity or athlete asked about their career, their life, or the mistakes that they've made, this seems to be the go-to answer. But I'm skeptical. How can that be? We all fall short of perfection so there must be something in that person's past that they regret. Maybe it's just me but I feel like there are thousands of decisions that I'd like to take back.

I know that a popular justification for not having any regrets, (or at least saying that you don't have any) is that every experience, decision, and action has made you who you are or brought you to the point where you are now. To a certain extent, that's true. I also get that as athletes, we are molded to have a rough and resilient disposition. Our emotional armor is such that we must exude toughness even when it comes to our past. Admitting that we made mistakes would only be admitting defeat. And in the arena of competitive athletics, that is simply unacceptable.

But it doesn't have to be. Admitting that you'd like to take something back—a decision, a shot attempt, or something you said—can be liberating. Holding back on admitting your regrets can take a toll on you. Maintaining that tough exterior isn't serving you in any way. In reality, it can have the opposite effect. It can keep you from taking the proper steps to a more maxed-out life. It will make you feel like you are not being true to yourself. Trying to constantly maintain the facade of not having any regrets can be exhausting. It's about being honest with yourself and telling yourself the truth.

Think of regret like this. If you are applying great pressure to a situation or attempting to accomplish something that you care about deeply (developing a relationship, for example), there are likely to be mistakes that occur along the way. In contrast, the less effort you put forth, the less messy it's likely to be, and the result will probably be fewer regrets. In other words, the more you care and are invested in a cause, the higher the potential for regret.

What if the parts of your past could actually become an asset? What if you could use those experiences as an opportunity to grow and become the person you know you want to become? Believing that you have no regrets is a cop-out. It's a way to avoid the necessary and sometimes difficult task of reflection. If you don't reflect, then you don't have to see a mistake or a weakness. After all, as athletes, we are trained to strive for perfection. Perfect practice and perfect performance. That's what gets results. But more than results and outcomes, I'd suggest that you chase growth. Growth is a long game. It can be painful at times, and it almost always requires work.

Pointing the magnifying glass on regrets isn't to beat ourselves up or obsess over the past. The objective is to ask yourself what you can learn from the regrets and how can that knowledge help you going forward into the future.

Try this: First, admit that you have some regrets. We all do. Next, write them down. Lay it all out in black and white on paper. Think about the four areas that these regrets may come from.

- Something you said
- Something you did
- Something you didn't say
- Something you didn't do

You'll find that this can be therapeutic and a way to take some of the weight off your shoulders. Maybe you'll find that you were even unaware that you were unnecessarily carrying around this excess baggage. Once you have them on paper, ask yourself if there's anything to be learned from them. How can they best be used to propel you forward? Now that you've seen the benefits of acknowledging regrets and you've decided to use them instead of letting them use you, there's one final step to moving forward.

Let them all go.

MEMENTO MORI

If the regrets of the past aren't holding you back, it's possible to get immersed in the uncertainty of what's to come in your future. Of course, none of us has a crystal ball or a time machine to see into the future (at least not yet!) And we can and should think about and plan, to the best of our ability, our futures.

Playing the "what if" game with ourselves, however, can be just as debilitating as looking backward. If you have just recently retired for good from your sport, there's no question you are experiencing a great deal of uncertainty. The last several years have most likely felt comfortable because of the certainty of your overall environment and what was likely to come next.

There is always comfort in what's familiar, but when things change, anxiety can hit like Aaron Donald in a contract year. *Where will I live? Where will I work? Is this all there is? What if I make a wrong decision that sets me back?* These are all natural questions to be asking. This never-ending loop has been called "paralysis by analysis." Too many thoughts, too many options and the idea that you have to have the rest of your time on earth figured out soon can lead to overwhelm. And when humans feel overwhelmed, a common by-product is avoidance or procrastination.

Fearing the future obviously takes away from the power of the present. And as with regret, worrying about whether it will all work out the way you hope can't be directly influenced by how much time and effort you spend thinking about the next three months or the next thirty years. How can you know? How can you say with any certainty what will happen? As much as we don't like to admit it to ourselves, a high number of factors are simply out of our control. And if you are like me, that's not a good feeling.

In 2015, after having a small hernia repaired in my right abdomen, I received some news that I wasn't expecting. It was supposed to just be a routine follow-up call. Hernias are pretty common, so I tried to ignore the pain and avoid the inconvenience of dealing with doctors and hospitals. I figured the time and headaches of scheduling doctor visits and all that came with those things weren't worth it. If avoiding those things meant dealing with a little discomfort every once in a while, then I could handle that. But when the pain persisted and the discomfort became noticeable to others, it was time to take some action.

The surgery was routine and took less than an hour to finish. A few weeks later, I had a CT scan to make sure everything was healing properly. In the days after the scan, I had mostly forgotten about it and didn't have any worries about the results of the surgery. But there was a small part of me that always feared what else the scan may have uncovered. Then the call came.

My heart started to beat a little faster as I pressed the play button on my cell's voicemail. *"Hi Bill, this is Doctor...."* Yeah, yeah, yeah.... *"We took a look at your scan...."* Come on...get to the point. *"Everything looks fine..."* So we're good? My brain was filtering everything out, frantically searching and waiting for the word "but." Then there it was.

"But the radiologists did find something else," he continued. "An aneurysm on your aorta." My worst fear about getting the hernia taken care of in the first place had become reality. I was terrified. I didn't know exactly what an aneurysm was, but I knew it sounded serious. There are certain medical terms and words in general that you just know aren't associated with anything good or positive. I knew *aneurysm* was one of those words.

The doctor tried to be reassuring and convince me that it wasn't anything that was worth getting worked up about. That it was just something that needed to be watched. But those words did very little to put me at ease. I went on a search for every morsel of information about aneurysms that I could find.

I know you're not supposed to get reassurance from a Google search, especially when it comes to health information. I dove in anyway. I wasn't looking for information as much as I was looking for hope. Maybe my perception of what an aneurysm is was inaccurate. I didn't major in medicine so there had to be a magic pill or procedure that would make this go away, right? And there is a viable solution for just about everything, isn't there? What I found out only made me feel worse.

I read articles about these bulges rupturing and people dying on their way to the hospital. I read about mortality rates and open heart procedures that come with dire complications. More articles about what the causes were and who is most at risk of developing an aneurysm filled my brain with chaos. I wasn't a smoker and was well under the average age of the average person who walks around with this condition. I was a healthy young person who still worked out religiously and who still considered himself an athlete. This must be happening to someone else. Why me? Am I going to die? My cage was rattled.

I'll never forget, as long as I live, the feeling that came over me at that moment while sitting on my bed. I was going to die. The realization felt like a right hook from Mike Tyson in his prime. Maybe not immediately, maybe not next week or next month, but my days on Earth were numbered. Finite. It was the first time I had felt the almost unbearable weight of my own mortality.

But there was something else. There was another feeling that overtook me in addition to the dread and the matter-of-fact nature of coming to grips with this wave of unwanted news. It was much heavier than the weight of the fact that I was going to die.

It was the overwhelming feeling that there was still so much more to accomplish before my time expired.

It literally took my breath away.

I knew with complete certainty in that moment that I had not come close to accomplishing everything that I wanted to yet. I knew that my accomplishments inside the arena were not enough. As great as some of those experiences were, if that's all that I did with my life, I wouldn't feel satisfied.

I still had unfinished business. There were beaches to walk with my wife. There was knowledge to pass on to my two children. There were experiences to share with people that I felt close to. Things yet to be discovered about myself. Books to read. Sunsets to watch. Things to create. People to impact. Meaning to be discovered.

When the aneurysm was initially discovered, doctors first prescribed an annual scan to check to see if it had grown at all in size. Once an aneurysm reaches a certain diameter, surgery is recommended to avoid the risk of rupture. After my doctors kept an eye on it for several years without any change, they extended the time in between checkups to two years. I'm happy to say that as I write these words, the aneurysm has not grown at all.

So I continue to live my life. But I now live it with a much different perspective. Instead of feeling sorry for myself, I am grateful that because of a routine hernia, doctors discovered this much more serious issue so now we can monitor it. Instead of thinking of it as a ticking time bomb, I use it as a reminder to be very selective with what I spend my time doing and thinking. Certain activities in my life have been drastically reduced or eliminated altogether. I hardly watch TV anymore (except for sports, of course.) And I ask myself these two important questions every day.

1. *If I knew I was going to die tomorrow, would I feel that I had accomplished a life full of meaning while using every drop of my potential?*
2. *What's one small thing I can do right now to ensure that when my time is up, the answer to the first question is "yes"?*

Memento Mori is Latin for "Remember you will die." Death is inevitable. This message isn't a morbid one. It's a positive reminder to get up every day with the view that you've been given the gift of another day to breathe. Embracing the idea of death will remind you to live. Ask yourself what you will do to make the days meaningful. Use it as a reminder that you have dreams that you still want to turn into reality. Use it to make better decisions. Use it as a tool to practice self-discipline. We have come to view death as something that we despise. We go to great lengths to avoid it. We are uncomfortable even talking about it, yet we are constantly rushing towards it.

Your time is running out. Regardless of your age, there is no getting around the fact that your days are numbered. And all your days matter. So do it now. Get busy. Whatever "it" is, get started now. No matter how small the thing is or how insignificant it may seem. Or how much time you think you may have to accomplish it. Call your parents and say thank you. Don't wait. You don't need a health issue or any other external factor to wake you out of the delusion that you have enough time. Let these words be your wake-up call. None of us know when our hourglass is going to run out of sand. Whether you are 18 or 88, you are moving closer to the end.

MAXIMIZE YOUR 1440

As difficult as it is to be an athlete, sometimes it's more excruciating to be a sports fan. I've been watching football games for years and after so many countless hours with my eyes glued to the action, I've noticed a few interesting patterns. Some of these patterns are physical, like the way tennis legend Rafael Nadal wipes the sweat from his face before each serve. Or how future Hall of Famer Aaron Rogers sometimes has both feet off the ground when he throws the ball.

Some distinctions can be chalked up to comfort or ritual, but other patterns fascinate me because of the basic connection to human nature. Isn't that why we love sports in the first place? The games are a lens through which we can observe the true essence of human behavior in various circumstances. What will they do when they are under pressure? How will they react when they have a big lead? How will they handle adversity or deal with success?

One of the more agonizing experiences that I've had as a fan is when the football team that I'm pulling for waits until right before the end of the first half or right before the end of the game to suddenly wake up, drive the ball down the field, and score. Usually, by this time, they've fallen behind and are now tasked with digging themselves out of a huge hole. And I'm left asking myself, "Why didn't they do this earlier?" In most cases, it's too late because they've run out of time. There are only so many minutes in each quarter or half of a football game.

Unlike our lives, the team has the luxury of knowing exactly how much time they have. And although they are aware of what is left on the clock, on some game days it gets wasted. Wasted by the illusion that there is enough time. Wasted by the subconscious thoughts of needing time to warm up and feel out the opposition. Wasted by the arrogance and ignorance that there is plenty of time.

181

I've been in their shoes as a player, so I know that sometimes even with the best effort, things can take a while to start clicking. It still is hard to understand why a team that has struggled for the better part of the half or the game only to make marching down the field quickly with precision and finesse look effortless.

Perhaps in these situations, there is something else at work. Maybe in that scenario, I'm watching the very *best* of human nature. That is the ability to respond when the chips are down, action needs to be taken and focus needs to be at its peak. I think I might also be witnessing human nature at its worst in these moments. Or at least a law of human nature.

Although we don't know how many days we have left to accomplish our big dreams, we do know how much time we get within *each* day that we are given. That number is 1,440. There are exactly 1,440 minutes in every day. We all get the same amount.

Some of us choose wisely while others aren't as good at distinguishing and identifying their big rocks, let alone prioritizing them. The choice to wait, to hesitate, to hold back, and to pay attention to the gravel and sand of life at the expense of what's most crucial and meaningful presents a dangerous risk, the risk of regret or wasting our present. It's one I'm not willing to take anymore.

So if we can't get a do-over on the past and we can't impact the future by worrying about it, what can we do? The first thing we need to realize is that time is the most precious asset we own. It's also one of the few things that we have control over.

The other is our thoughts. We can decide where to place our mental energy. I struggle with this on a daily basis. As I write this section, I am simultaneously thinking about what will come from this book being put out into the world. I could write an entire book on just those questions and worries alone. Who will want to read these words? Aren't these ideas and concepts that I'm writing about obvious? Am I wasting my time? Should I call it quits and go watch March Madness instead?

Try this next time you lose sight of the present moment and go down a rabbit hole of feeling anxious about your future or what will happen in the near or distant future. Make the most of your time by losing track of it. Do something that forces you to focus on that specific thing. Find a flow activity that allows you to immerse yourself in it and it alone. Are you thinking of one now? For me, trying to figure out the lyrics of certain songs or lifting heavy weights requires me to concentrate intensely.

The present moment is all we have. How deep we can get into it and fully appreciate it is a tough skill to master, and I haven't yet met anyone who has successfully conquered this practice. But if time is the most valuable and fleeting treasure that we own, shouldn't we be spending it on now?

In the next chapter, we'll look at some specific actions we can take to create daily routines to maximize our 1440 and take one step at a time across the canyon.

Stick Your Hand in the Fire

- What do you want to avoid regretting when you look back at this exact moment three years from now? Five years? Twenty-five years?

> "Enjoy all you have while pursuing all you want."
>
> —Jim Rohn

11

HARNESS THE BLAZE

No one gave us a chance.

It had already been determined, even days before the game had begun. In the eyes of the college football world, we had already lost to the #1 ranked Ohio State Buckeyes. The experts were so sure of what the outcome would be that we were pegged as 28-point underdogs. The game would be played on the road and late in the season when it is obvious which teams are good and which ones are not. Our team was 4-4, very inconsistent and we didn't know what our identity was.

Some teams begin the season ranked highly by the pollsters then quickly drop after a few games when it becomes apparent they are pretenders and not contenders. Ohio State had been the preseason #1 ranked team, had been dominant all year, and never slipped out of the top spot. It was assumed by most that they would play for a national championship at the end of that season.

As players and competitors, you go into every game thinking and believing you can win. You have to. Without that attitude, you simply have no shot. But we weren't delusional either. We knew what we were up against. Ohio State was talented, deep at every position, and well-coached. More importantly, they were confident. The kind of confidence that comes from knowing that you've had consistent success in the past and you can replicate that success every time you suit up to play.

Nick Saban, our head coach, was different during the practice week leading up to the game. Normally, you could feel the pressure he felt to obtain the desired outcome when the game was over: to win. After all, that's why you play, isn't it? That's the goal. But this week, the vibe was different. The message was different. Maybe it was because he knew that our chances of reaching that outcome were slim. We had some talented players who would eventually go on to have careers in the NFL, but there was no cohesion, no consistency. We weren't a *team* yet.

He talked to us about how we were going to mentally approach that week of practice knowing that we had a tall task ahead of us. It was to be a sort of experiment. If there ever was a week to try a novel approach, this was it. He explained that we weren't going to be focused on the outcome. We weren't going to be looking at the scoreboard. Doing so would only bring tension and anxiety. We would instead have a hyper-focus on doing the things necessary to play the best football that we could play. Each player would only focus on what he needed to do on that singular next play, not worrying or thinking about future plays, scores, or any other factors outside of his control.

The goal wouldn't be to win the game, but instead to win the next six seconds. And he would direct all his concentration, effort, toughness, and energy towards that one play. No matter what the result of that particular play was, we would line up and have the same approach on the next one. Done throughout the game, for the entire game, this strategy would allow us to be at peace with the results whether they ended up in our favor or not.

Psychologically detaching from the outcome allowed us to remove the pressure of trying to control some future event. Because we became driven by the *process* of what steps it took to achieve a goal instead of the goal itself, the outcome of that game was unexpected. We won 28-24.

Taking your eyes off the scoreboard takes the pressure off. More importantly, it brings into focus the only things that matter. What can you do on a daily basis that moves you closer to your goals? What consistent, repeatable habits will alleviate the pressure of the future while optimizing your perspective in the present moment?

PROCESS DRIVEN

Your process for achieving any objective, goal, or ambition, no matter how small, is the bridge between where you are now and where you want to be. In Part Three, you established your goals. What's the easiest and most sure-fire way to get there? Have a process. Remember, no matter how hard you try, you can't control the outcome. But you can control what you focus on. You can control the process. Those tiny little doable actions that will slowly but surely move you down the field are what require your focus.

Let's consider just a few of those daily actions you can take to stoke the flames and move toward who you are becoming.

MORNING ROUTINE

While there are several benefits of not leaving the most important part of your day—the beginning—to chance, here are a handful of keys to owning the day because you chose to start it with a routine. I like to refer to having a morning routine as "playing with a lead."

A lot has been made of having a morning routine, and it's often pointed out that most successful leaders, entrepreneurs, CEOs, etc.

have a rock-solid schedule of actions they perform each morning. It's not about trying to imitate those people, though. Everyone's lives and goals (and mornings) are unique. The key is to start the day *deliberately*.

I have a confession to make. Until less than two years ago, I wasn't a morning person. I used to have one of those coffee mugs that indicated when I'd be ready to talk to you based on how much coffee was left in the cup. I wanted to get up when I was ready or when some extenuating circumstance (like my kids needing to be fed) forced me to.

Today, I couldn't operate properly without my morning routine. It has evolved a bit as I've learned and paid attention to what works for me and what doesn't. And I'm sure it will evolve as I create new ambitions, but here is what it looks like now.

5:00 a.m. Wake up

5:05 a.m. Make coffee

5:20 a.m. Focus on 3 things I'm grateful for

              Read/write my list of affirmations

              Visualize my Anchor List for ten minutes

5:30 a.m. Write/Create

6:30 a.m. Make breakfast for the kids

7:30 a.m. Take kids to school

We'll look at some of these steps in more detail in this chapter. Again, this is just one person's routine. The point is to make the routine your own and to create a morning ritual that lets you get your most important stuff in before the day runs away from you.

GRATITUDE

Thank you. These two words have the power to change the way you think about the struggles you currently face. With so much uncertainty about what the future holds for you, it can be easy to disconnect entirely from what you currently have, what you've already experienced, and what you've learned up to this point. While the objective is to create a new path and new meaning by creating your future self, it's important not to overlook what you've already been given and what you already possess. Whether you are thanking a friend, parent, coach, teammate, God, or yourself, taking time to say those words can be life-changing.

Athletes are programmed to think about the next step. You have been wired to focus on what you have yet to conquer. There is still so much to look forward to. You have new dreams, ambitions, and surprises that await you tomorrow and years into the future. These are all great things, even the trials that you will face. But they all can also lead to a deep sense of lack.

What you don't yet have and what you don't have right now can create a feeling of discontent, especially as you fall into the comparison trap of what your friends are doing and how some former teammates seem to have things figured out already. Regardless of your current situation, there is abundance in your life. But with such a strong focus on the future, the treasures of the present tend to get lost.

What is gratitude?

Athletes receive a ton of recognition. In fact, that's one of the things many athletes struggle with the most once their careers end. There aren't enough boosts to the ego once the applause fades. Like in other areas, there is an abundance of praise during your career and very little when you're no longer achieving big things inside the arena. Outsiders are appreciating you and all the things you're doing well. Fans may thank you for an autograph or tell you how much they enjoyed watching your last game. Emotionally, it can be a great deal easier to receive rather than give.

If you're feeling like you're not enough anymore to feel appreciated, it might be time to become the one doing the recognizing. Gratitude is really nothing more than a commitment to yourself to be aware enough to recognize that something good has happened to you. Big and small things happen to you every day that give you the opportunity to be grateful. You opened your eyes this morning after a good night's sleep in a warm bed. You breathe fresh air. You ate today. There is someone in your life who cares about your happiness and success. Gratitude is an appreciation that something that you value in your life has happened to you. And these things generally go way beyond superficial things that only have financial value.

Robert Emmons, the world's leading expert on gratitude research, contends that there are two main parts of gratitude. First, he believes that when you become conscious of those valuable things that you're grateful for, you "affirm that there are good things in the world, gifts and benefits we've received." The second component is that "we recognize that the sources of this goodness are outside of ourselves."

Experiences, places visited, random occurrences, and gifts from others all can be appreciated and acknowledged. Reading a little more into the second part of this definition makes me think of the people that I am grateful for having had an influence on me at some point along my path. I am grateful, of course, for my parents. My coaches and teammates give me a deep sense of gratitude. Not only for helping me reach my goals but because of the connection and the relationships formed. There are countless others who had nothing to gain by helping me or wanting me to succeed. Their unselfishness is humbling. I am grateful for all of them. Without them, I wouldn't be writing this book.

There is, though, a potentially tough element to gratitude for many athletes. During your time as a competitor, there were many mantras repeated to you over and over literally thousands of times to motivate you to push yourself past your limits. One of those popular athlete mantras is "You gotta earn it." It can be challenging to acknowledge and appreciate all those things in your life that you have that *didn't* come through hard work. What things do you have that came to you without you having to earn them? Focus on those and be grateful.

Benefits of gratitude

"Life doesn't happen to you; it happens for you." This quote by the accomplished actor Jim Carey cuts right to the heart of what gratitude can do for you. The mistake we athletes can make is to not see what's right in front of our faces. So you too may be asking yourself some questions that lead to dead ends. *Why is this happening to me?* is a natural response to the problem at hand. However, a slight shift in how you view the problem will instantly change your outlook on why this is happening to you. This trial, this test, exists as another problem you get to solve. Be grateful for the challenge. And the courage to face it head-on.

In addition to a change in perspective, there are many other proven benefits to a concentration on the good that surrounds you. Here are my top four:

Physical Health

This one should speak to you instantly. Athletes know the importance of remaining in great physical shape. Your career ending doesn't mean your body is less important. You might not have a competition to train for but you do have to take care of your physical health so you are as prepared as possible for the biggest endurance test one can undertake—living a rich and meaningful life that will last not minutes or hours, but decades.

Improving your physical health through gratitude doesn't require that you spend hours at the gym or even break a sweat. While gratitude might not change the shape of your body, it can protect the parts of your body that you can't see. In a 2015 study, researchers at the University of California, San Diego, found that gratitude can improve the health of your heart. It doesn't get any more important than that.

Reduces Stress

No one likes to feel the effects of stress. When you are under pressure, your heart rate increases, you may start to sweat, and you run the risk of losing focus on what is going to produce the best results for you. Having a grateful outlook can reduce the stress and anxiety you feel about your future. Regulating your emotions and not losing your cool in tough moments is critical in many situations. What if there was a quick trick to guarding against letting those emotions get the best of you? Gratitude can be the answer.

In a 2017 study, researchers from Seoul, Korea, discovered that when the participants focused on things they were grateful for, their heart rates went down and the parts of the brain associated with anxiety flare-ups tended to calm down as well. All of this suggests that when in the throes of a stressful time, focusing your attention and your mental energy on something you are thankful for can drastically reduce the symptoms associated with stress. When you are experiencing the strong emotions of stress, sadness, or depression, the other parts of the brain responsible for reason, logic, and good decision-making shut down.

Strengthens Relationships

Relationships matter. They will be as meaningful to your post-career success as anything else. You know that working with teammates, while ultimately rewarding, is not without its challenges. Whether you're working with teammates to get a win over your rival or working with your spouse on how to best parent your child through a challenging time at school, there's bound to be a time where you butt heads or get on each other's nerves. Merely spending an extraordinary amount of time with others can lead to irritation and miscommunication. These tensions can start to fracture the relationship which could cost you one of the most meaningful parts of your existence. But the more you focus on the good things that the people in your life bring to the table, the stronger your relationships will be. Recognizing the good in others will cultivate empathy in you.

Better Sleep

Gratitude can improve sleep quality by promoting relaxation. When you practice gratitude, it activates the area of the brain that's associated with reward and positive emotions, which can lead to lower levels of anxiety about the future. This in turn makes it easier for you to fall asleep and stay asleep. Not only that, but gratitude can help you be more focused on the present allowing for a more restful night's sleep. Practicing gratitude by reflecting on the positive experiences from your day right before you go to bed can be a game-changer in terms of the quality of sleep that you receive. Sleep is underrated and often taken for granted when you think of your overall health. The type of day you have tomorrow starts with the quality of your sleep tonight.

Much like your athletic transformations, these benefits don't simply appear. They must be practiced over and over until the effects stack on top of each other.

AFFIRMATIONS

"I am the type of person that takes care of my body."

This is not only a personal and true statement, it's an affirmation that I repeat to myself daily. Why? Because I was once an athlete who wasn't as aware of what I was putting into my body or conscious of the negative effects those things were having on my health. I've always been the type of person who could eat whatever I wanted and not gain a pound. (I know this is the opposite problem most people have, so feel free to pause for a quick eye roll.) Because of my metabolic good fortune, I spent years trying to gain weight to become a bigger, stronger, and better athlete by inhaling double cheeseburgers and milkshakes full of sugar without a second thought. More calories were all I was after and without the proper nutrition education, I ate whatever I could get my hands on and whatever sounded good in the moment.

Now removed from my playing days and much more educated on what certain foods and drinks can do to a body, you'd think that would be all it would take to keep me away from a salted caramel doughnut or a heaping bowl of Lucky Charms. Temptation tests my discipline every day, and some days my discipline needs backup. That's why I have enlisted the power of affirmations to keep me away from the bags of Doritos. More importantly, affirmations are powerful reminders of the type of person I want to become.

What are affirmations and how do they work?

Affirmations are positive statements that people repeat to themselves (or write down) to help them change their thinking patterns and behavior. You may have used affirmations during your playing days to help you prepare for a game or a practice. The thinking behind using affirmations is that, by repeating positive statements, people rewire their brains for achievement and ultimate success.

There have been several scientific studies that suggest that affirmations may be effective in helping you achieve your goals and dreams. One study published in the *Journal of Experimental Social Psychology* found that people who repeated positive affirmations were more likely to take action toward their goals and exhibited more persistence in the face of setbacks.

Potential benefits of using affirmations

In addition to linking your goals and dreams to the daily, required actions needed to accomplish them, affirmations have a number of other positive benefits.

- **Increased positivity and self-esteem**: Repeating affirmations can help shift negative self-talk and increase feelings of self-worth and confidence.
- **Improved motivation and focus**: Affirmations can help boost motivation and encourage a greater focus on goals.
- **Enhanced resilience and coping skills**: Affirmations can help you build resilience and develop stronger coping skills in the face of challenges and setbacks.

Success with affirmations requires commitment, practice, and an open mind.

VISUALIZATION

Mental practice can get you closer to who you want to become. In some cases, it can be almost as effective as the physical equivalent of what you are trying to accomplish. The process of visually rehearsing certain actions can have a profound effect on actually performing that particular act or becoming the thing you imagine.

One mind-blowing example of this comes from a study conducted at the Lerner Research Institute in Cleveland, Ohio. Researchers found that visualizing gaining muscle strength is almost as productive as actually lifting weights to get stronger. (Wait, what? Had I known that I could've at least made a strong case to my coach as to why I should be exempt from those 6:00 a.m. lifting sessions.) The activated brain patterns of the athletes who lifted 100 pounds were similar to those patterns that came from simply imagining lifting the same amount of weight.

If the mind can be that powerful to influence physical strength, imagine what visualization can do to move you toward your goals. In the previous chapters, you started to dream about the next, future version of you. Seeing yourself as *being that person already* through the continual practice of visualizing has to become a part of your new workout routine.

Your in-house search engine

Fortunately, there is a device that can help you. It can enhance your own power of visualization, but it doesn't require a hard drive or a battery or even a search box. It already resides in your brain. The reticular activating system (RAS) is a part of the brain that acts as a filter for incoming information. It plays an important role in determining which pieces of information are important enough to be processed and acted upon.

One way that the RAS relates to visualization is the ability to amplify certain stimuli in your environment while suppressing others. When you actively visualize something in your mind, you can stimulate the RAS to focus on those mental images and to help them become more visible and tangible. This means you already possess a powerful tool for enhancing creativity, problem-solving, and goal-setting, as it allows you to effectively engage with your imagination and bring your ideas to life.

Have you ever wanted to own a certain type of car? Cadillac? Porsche? What happens when you start to focus on that one particular car? You start seeing them everywhere. You notice them on the highway and in parking lots. Everywhere you go, they pop up. Not only that, but you notice the hundreds of other cars less. Once you set your mental filter, your RAS starts to do its thing.

The RAS can also help you filter out distractions and negative thoughts while you visualize which can make the process more efficient and effective. By training the RAS to focus on the more positive aspects of our mental imagery, you can build stronger pathways in your brain that reinforce your goals and help you achieve them more easily. Overall, understanding how the RAS works can be a valuable tool for any former athlete looking to search for the things, experiences, and people that you want to invite into your life. The RAS is easily accessible to everyone who wants to use it to visualize themselves in the future during such an uncertain period in their lives.

TRACKING

If you are going to play with a lead, you have to know what the score is. In this case, though, you are not competing against an opponent or measuring an outcome. You're only tracking the process of a few simple daily rituals that will get you some practice in changing what you see and how you feel about yourself and your future. Like with any new skill, it must be developed over time and not ignored or practiced only sporadically. What you focus on expands, and what's important should be tracked. What gets tracked gets done, and what gets done produces results.

Jerry Seinfeld is probably best known for creating one of America's most popular TV sitcoms of all time. From 1989 to 1998, *Seinfeld* ran on NBC and was must-see TV for fans of Jerry, Kramer, George, and Elaine. After he decided to not continue creating the show, he was offered 100 million dollars to continue but turned it down, instead opting to walk away from the show at the height of its popularity.

Seinfeld began his career in New York as a stand-up comedian in the 1970s. As an up-and-comer, he had only one objective—to write one joke every day. Not a mind-blowing monologue or enough material for an hour-long stand-up special. Just one joke. It didn't matter how good or bad the joke was. He judged his success on writing that singular joke every day.

Seinfeld had a big calendar that he hung on his wall and for every day that he wrote, he put a big red "X" through that date. It wasn't long before he had a few X's in a row. It became a visual reminder of the progress he was making and the work he was putting in. He also gave this advice to a young comedian who asked him for advice. He said that if you want to be a better comedian, you need better jokes. And better jokes come from writing every day. The trick was to just keep chipping away and your chain will start to grow. After a while, your mind will become consumed with not breaking that chain, not some future outcome. Don't break the chain.

Obviously, this simple system can be used for any habit that you want to start, maintain, or eliminate. For me, I've chosen to use Seinfeld's system to focus my thoughts on the right things. Gratitude, affirmation, and visualizing who I want to become are now the most crucial elements of my day. I practice them in the morning and the impact this has on the rest of my day is epic. It didn't have noticeable effects right away, but I have changed the way I think about myself, my place in the world, and what I want my future to look like.

I couldn't imagine myself not engaging with this quick and simple process every single day. It's easy to do, but also easy not to do as well. When life happens and my morning gets disrupted, I always find some time before the day ends to make sure this practice gets done. The results then take care of themselves and show up as more patience with my family, a better outlook on the world, and more positivity. Put in the reps and you will be rewarded.

Stick Your Hand in the Fire

- What does your process look like?
- What are you grateful for?
- What's one affirmation that you can create to help you become the person you want to be?
- Can you see your future self? Your future life? Do you practice feeling the emotion attached to the future version of you?

"Don't ask what the world needs. Ask what makes you come alive and go do it. Because what the world needs is people who have come alive."

—Howard Thurman

12

EXPLODE EXPECTATIONS

It was supposed to be fun. And it was, for a while. Less than a year after my career ended, I decided it was time to do something I had never done before. Whitewater rafting sounded like a good time, so I polled a few friends to see if they'd be into it. It didn't take much arm-twisting before we had a crew together and an adventure to look forward to.

I was living in my hometown of Warren, Ohio, so the closest rafting destination was Ohiopyle State Park, located in southwestern Pennsylvania. The focal point of the park and the region is the Youghiogheny River, which boasts some of the best whitewater rafting in the U.S. Since I had never been rafting before, I didn't know what an attractive place it was for rafting enthusiasts.

The scenery alone was worth the two-and-a-half-hour drive. Towering bridges over the river that connected peaks of the mountains, rolling hills, and of course, the rushing sounds of the water hitting the rocks all lived up to the vision I had in my head. Sunny blue skies were the icing on the cake. When my career ended,

I didn't realize what a dropoff there would be in the areas of excitement and new experiences.

A few times during the trip down the river, the guides would pull everyone over to the shore at a calm spot on the river to give some quick additional guidance as to the best way to navigate the next set of rapids. We would all nod, take in the information, and eagerly get back to the action of paddling to the next hit of dopamine. During one of those pit stops, the guide had something extra to offer.

He mentioned how there was a bit of extra skill involved in navigating the upcoming set of rapids and said that if we wanted to step onto shore and carry our raft around this point in the river, that option was available. Several groups decided to take that route, but it didn't take long for ours to quickly decide that we would not be taking the easy path. If we traveled that distance for a new and exciting experience, we wanted the full experience.

What made this particular segment of rapids so challenging was a massive rock, half below the water's surface and half protruding up from the river, staring rafters in the face and directly in the path of where the strong current was pushing you to go. The guide gave us a paddling plan and detailed techniques to navigate around the huge rock looming out of the river.

Positioned at the far left of the river, it stood opposite other small rocks that created a curved opening that required precise timing and a little luck to maneuver around it. The way to successfully sidestep the rock and avoid a collision with it was to paddle right at it, turn the raft parallel with the rock, then paddle hard to the middle of the river and clear the rock before colliding with it. Once to the right of the boulder, the current would take you past the toughest section and let you catch your breath. It sounded simple enough. We watched as the other group successfully made it look easy. After all, there was a guide standing on the top of the rock that would be reminding us of what to do and when to do it.

We were either going to nail it, or we were going to get wet. Whatever the outcome, we were going to know in a matter of a few seconds because it was our turn to start paddling our way towards the slab of stone. As we approached the rock, we managed to turn our boat parallel to the rock. Step one was successful. However, the all-important second step was where we fell short. Because of the force of the current pushing us straight ahead and our inexperience, we just couldn't get far enough to the right of the rock, and we smashed into it. What happened next was the scariest moment of my life.

The raft tipped backward and dumped all six members of our group into the river. Four of the six spilled out to the right of the rock and the current took them down the middle of the river, which was where our boat was supposed to end up, with all of us in it and smiles on our faces. My friend Tom and I, who were positioned on the back of the raft, hit the water and were immediately pinned against the underwater portion of the rock by the raging current. I struggled urgently to find a path to the surface, but the force of the current felt like an older brother who was using his knee to hold his younger sibling on the ground. I tried to the left and then to the right but to no avail.

Given that one of the requirements of playing the position of quarterback was to be able to control my emotions in tense situations, I remained calm and was confident that the situation would resolve itself quickly. In what must have been a millisecond, though, I went from thinking I had ice water in my veins to thinking the ice-cold current on my skin would be the last sensation I'd ever experience. I was now in full panic mode. I wasn't able to move, and I was running out of ideas.

I don't know why, but as I tried to move one more time, I was thrust to the water's surface and greeted by the mixed sounds of screams and rushing water. Ropes were being tossed into the river by guides along the shore as a lifeline to safety. The other rafters could only watch as the scene went from serene to chaotic in the blink of an eye. I was spit out to the left of the rock, so I was able to quickly step onto the bank of the river and plop down on the dirt. Tom was pushed out to the right and down the middle of the river where he was able to grab a rope as well. I mumbled "What just happened?" to myself as I struggled to process the last few seconds.

Sometime later, I would discover that the imposing rock that almost took my life, (and that of my best friend Tom), had a name: Dimple Rock. Usually, things are awarded nicknames because there is a degree of significance to them. Fame becomes the result of attention. In this case, however, infamy was the cause of all the articles and news coverage of the gigantic tank-like slab of stone. From 1976-2000, seventeen lives were lost in that area of the river. Just a year before our experience, three people died in one summer. This was the early 2000's so the internet wasn't quite the ever-present behemoth it is today, and we certainly weren't carrying it around in our pockets. So somehow the research element of the adventure slipped past us, and we were left rushing toward a dangerous rock without the knowledge of the lives that had already been lost there over the years.

In the years following the incident, I didn't spend that much time focusing on the meaning of it, if there was a meaning at all. I chalked it up to a tense moment in the middle of an otherwise fun experience. There's a certain perceived invincibility that comes with being in your early twenties and I think my experience as an athlete taught me to always be looking forward to what's next. *Forget about the last play, focus on the next one.*

Although I didn't realize it then, the light bulb went on some years later. Maybe I didn't die that day because there is more work to be done. More relationships to be cultivated. More lessons to be learned. More people to impact. More questions to be asked. More life to live.

In the years that I was an athlete, and especially in the months and years immediately after it ended, I couldn't shake the nagging feeling that somehow the universe screwed up. I was *supposed* to be an athlete. That's what all the signs in my life pointed to. So that's what I was *expecting* to continue to be.

So when my playing days came to a close, I felt as if the universe hadn't held up its end of the deal. A promise had been broken. But as I would later learn from cracking open Frankl's book about his experiences in a concentration camp over a half-century earlier, what I expected from life didn't matter. It didn't matter that I wanted to continue to perform in front of thousands of fans and get paid handsomely for it. It didn't matter that I wanted to stay in my comfort zone and do what came naturally to me. What did matter was what life expected from me.

What does life expect from you? Whether you know it or not, life is asking you questions. And not just the big ones that seem to only surface once in a while, but also the little ones that occur every hour of the day. What if your career wasn't the end? What if it was just the beginning? What if instead of your playing days being the climax of your existence, they were the kickoff of something far more significant?

RESPONSIBILITY

One thing life expects of you is to take seriously your responsibility to chase what is meaningful for you and to discover what your life means. No one is coming to save you. You are no longer on scholarship, so to speak. Your purpose is to find the meaning of your life for you. You may not have been the reason your career came to a close. Countless athletes are forced to retire from their sport because of an injury or some other extenuating circumstance. Like it or not though, you are now responsible for creating the solution for yourself. You are responsible for picking up the pieces.

Duty. Obligation. A state of being answerable. Responsibility is not just the ability to respond, but the *desire* to respond. It's an understanding and a willingness that you have to carry that burden on your shoulders. Will you answer the call? Will you respond, and if so, how? Responsibility means stepping into the darkness of uncertainty with your head up and your eyes wide open, not fully knowing the path or what waits for you on it.

Remember in Chapter 5 when we talked about your unfair advantages? Those are born from a uniqueness that only you can own. The same can be said for your responsibility.

> *"When the impossibility of replacing a person is realized, it allows the responsibility which a man has for his existence and its continuance to appear in all its magnitude. A man who becomes conscious of the responsibility he bears toward a human being who affectionately waits for him, or to an unfinished work, will never be able to throw away his life. He knows the 'why' for his existence, and he will be able to bear almost any 'how'.*
>
> Victor Frankl, Man's Search for Meaning.

I know that you can—and believe that you will—choose to accept responsibility for pursuing and creating the meaning in your life. As with almost everything else in life, there are benefits of doing the thing and consequences of not doing the thing.

HOPE

You may have heard the expression that hope is not a strategy. While that is true, it is vital to focus on how bright the future could be and who you could become next. Imagine going to the gym and genuinely thinking that you will never get into the shape that you want to achieve. Or beginning every game that you played thinking that you would never achieve victory. I've found in my experience that hope is one of the most powerful driving forces in my life.

Before we move on, though, I want to emphasize that *blind* hope can be a recipe for a stack of regrets and wasted time. What is blind hope? It's hope and nothing else. Hope doesn't play an individual sport. It only works with teammates. And its favorite teammate is action. Hope without action is merely a wish. And nothing great was ever accomplished by only wishing for it.

In the movie, *The Shawshank Redemption,* the main character Andy Dufresne is wrongfully imprisoned and openly talks about his dreams of seeing the blue waters of the Pacific Ocean and living a normal life again one day. The other prisoners warn Andy about the dangers of hope. With one of the most famous quotes from the movie, Andy replies "Hope is a good thing, maybe the best of things, and no good thing ever dies." Would Andy have ever achieved his dream of seeing the ocean again if he hadn't spent several years chipping away at the tunnel he later used as his escape? He was focused on a future goal even though everyone told him it was impossible. He never gave up hope.

The ability for all of us to focus on a future goal because it gives us the hope that better days are ahead. It gives us the hope we can push forward when times seem impossible. Hope is not a delusion;

it is what fills us with optimism that tomorrow can be a better day and that we can reach our dreams. It's not meant to take us away from the hard work that's necessary to get there.

If hopelessness is the cause of anxiety and depression, it would stand to reason that hope is the driver for the very strong belief that anything is possible for our lives. Without hope, we stand still, we don't move forward, and we freeze because we don't believe that there are brighter days ahead. So we don't grind, scratch, claw, and push through the hurdles of fear and doubt because we don't believe that it's worth it. But it absolutely is.

Without hope, the flame starts to flicker. Former athletes face hopelessness when the focus is not clear and there is no action to partner with the hope. At times it seems like you are crawling through the dark night not knowing what awaits on the other side of the muck you sometimes have to fight through. But hope is where you start. It's what pulls you out of bed on days when your planner is blank. It's why you allow yourself to believe that there might be something good coming even if you don't fully believe it yet.

Hope is also the precursor to courage.

COURAGE

If you're reading this, you're no stranger to courage. Overcoming obstacles, playing through pain because your team needed you, fearlessly taking the last shot, and taking the blame for a difficult loss are all signs of courage. Think back to before your career began. Can you recall your first courageous act?

It most likely wasn't any of the valiant actions mentioned above. It was the choice to step inside the arena in the first place. You stepped forward to see what you were made of. Despite the risk of physical harm or the shame of defeat, you went in anyway. You didn't know what was in store for you, but something called you to move. So you went.

Are you ready to do it again? Just as you had the courage to step into the arena that first time, do you have the courage to step into a new arena?

"I learned that courage was not the absence of fear," Nelson Mandela once said, "but the triumph over it. The brave man is not he who does not feel afraid, but he who conquers that fear." This embodies not only the essence of what it takes to be a competitive athlete, but what it now takes to answer life's call to you.

Courage to let go

When it's time to move on, you may be confronted with attachments that conflict with or prevent you from evolving. The desire to rekindle an interest in a hobby you had years before you started your sport or a curiosity about exploring a different part of the country. You may want to step into something on the complete opposite of the spectrum from sports, but friends roll their eyes at you when you tell them about it. *You* may be the one holding you back from letting go of past attachments. You've fit yourself into a category, an identity. Competitor. Warrior. Champion. Hustler. Survivor. Athlete.

The identity that you built provided stability and security and was cultivated over years. Letting that go can not only feel uncomfortable, but downright scary. It can feel like you're saying goodbye to a part of you that has died. It will take courage to know that you will survive. It will take courage to believe that you can embrace your past while leaving it in the rear-view mirror.

Courage to be yourself

Being yourself means having the courage to express your true thoughts, feelings, and ideas with conviction but without shame or the fear of rejection or judgment. Not easy to do. This becomes easier when you know yourself well enough to exude the confidence in who you are.

My confidence had come from my identity as an athlete. When my career ended, I discovered that I didn't know who I was. I didn't know what I believed. I didn't know what I wanted. I only knew myself as I had always known myself—as an athlete. All the things that went along with that. Who was I without the core of who I was to others and myself? I didn't have a clue. So the quest began.

No one can beat you at being you. But no one will know or appreciate who you truly are unless you know who that person is first.

Courage to be vulnerable

Today, more than ever, you need to have the courage to be vulnerable. This is difficult for most athletes and is another trait that needs to be unlearned over time. The arena asked you to be tough, avoid showing weakness, and emotionally muscle yourself through adversity. There wasn't time or room to be tired, soft, or weak. There are times as an athlete when it's not acceptable to be sick. You were needed in the arena. You were expected to show up at one hundred percent—both physically and mentally—whether that was actually the case or not.

Now, a different approach is not only possible, but welcomed. It might just be one of your most valuable assets if you can use it for good. Genuine vulnerability is one of the things that makes you human. It will allow you to relate to others, become approachable, and ultimately connect on a deeper level with those around you.

Vulnerability is all about being open and trusting that things will work out.

There will be many new experiences ahead and some of those will bring with them the discomfort of not knowing how things will turn out or the potential of falling flat on your face. The ability to push aside that fear of not knowing or looking like a beginner may just be the thing that pushes you ahead. To those who never played a sport, athletes can seem indestructible. Nerves of steel wrapped in a body built to withstand punishment. But it's the courage to be vulnerable that allows others to connect with you on a deeper level, and that vulnerability will serve as your greatest strength.

MISSION

Fighter pilots embark on dangerous missions into enemy territory. Maybe it is a mission simply to collect information, to protect the country's citizens, or to protect land. While the goal of the mission is clearly laid out, often the *outcome* of the mission is completely uncertain.

Various organizations set out on mission trips to foreign lands to try and do their part to make the world a better place in some way. Astronauts spend years planning, studying, testing, and revising ways to learn what we don't yet know about worlds beyond our own. Details are ironed out, plans are made, and ideas are vetted along with best practices and what's failed in the past. There are leaders of the mission and supporters who are inspired by the vision of the leaders.

One thing all these people and groups have in common is the very simple act of putting others' interests before their own. Their greatest mission, other than the task at hand, is serving others. Pilots aren't thinking about themselves as they fly into the danger zone. They are called to look outside of themselves and accept the risk involved to serve a bigger cause. Missionaries sacrifice luxury and time, and may even risk their own lives, to reach people in dangerous parts of the world who need their help. Astronauts launch themselves outside of the earth's atmosphere and test the very limits of what's possible for humans, all in the name of knowledge and advancement for the human race.

One of the surest ways to kill your suffering and the sense of loss from your sport no longer being the center of who you are is through service to others. Whether you are experiencing a sense of uncertainty about your own future, your immediate problems that feel like the weight of the world is sitting on your shoulders, or the pressure to have it all figured out before attempting to leave your mark, consider giving. Consider getting outside of yourself. Get out of your own head and dive into the myriad of ways that you can be of service to others.

In the book *The Go Giver,* authors Bob Burg and John David Mann state that the most valuable gift you can offer someone is yourself. It's called the Law of Authenticity. You don't need to risk your life or change the world. But you just might change the world of one person.

Your mission is not only to discover your unique gifts but to offer them up in service to someone other than yourself. As an athlete, you tied your identity to your sport even though you knew you wouldn't be able to play forever. You knew that at some point, your situation was going to change. The clock on your career was going to run out. But when the time comes and the change takes place, you are still left disoriented.

The other major life change that I've experienced that I couldn't have been fully prepared for was when I became a parent. I had heard other parents advise that there was never going to be a time when I felt fully prepared to take on the very big responsibility of being a dad. Talk about feeling disoriented!

One solution is to identify a personal mission statement, not necessarily to share with the outside world, although you could. Instead, establish those things at your core that don't change when your circumstances do. When this statement is in place, it can provide meaning to you when your surroundings are unsettling, uncomfortable, or unfamiliar.

In a weird and interesting twist, I discovered the basis for my statement during my brief time with those same New York Giants that told me that there wasn't a spot on the team for me there. Before the pre-season games, chapel services were made available to us. I attended one before the last game before I was cut. At the end of the short session, the chaplain closed with a prayer that asked for *perseverance, patience,* and *peace.*

If you haven't realized it yet, I'm a fan of alliteration. It makes things easy to remember. For some reason, those three words stuck with me not only as I walked out of the service, but to this day. I later would add the words *perspective* and *purpose* for a statement that is anchored by five simple words that all start with the same letter. I call the statement **The Player's Proclamation**.

> *I am ready for what may come, knowing that I'm committed to keeping those things within the larger perspective of my life. I will pursue a purpose greater than myself that is driven by constant perseverance balanced with a calm patience. I accept that there may be challenges and triumphs, and the anticipation of both serves to deliver peace.*

Perspective. Purpose. Perseverance. Patience. Peace

LEGACY

How do you want to be remembered? Have you thought about it? If not, you should. Will the word "athlete" be used first, last, or not at all to describe you once your story comes to a conclusion?

Uncovering your mission, then setting off on the path to build it, one step at a time, all while learning and growing along the way will bring an unfathomable amount of satisfaction and fulfillment for you. Of course, in serving others you'll be giving to others who need your gifts, experience, and knowledge.

But your mission will serve an important additional purpose: a legacy. Yes, your athletic career may have been significant enough to reach and impact a multitude of fans who derived entertainment and memories from your performances. However, can you do more? Can you serve people in a way that is beneficial for them? Will that service last long after you're gone?

Even while they are still playing, most of your athletic heroes have chosen to get involved in charitable organizations to give back and use their platform to create a ripple effect and a lasting impact on others. For the causes they believe in, they not only donate money but their time as well. Some take it a step further and create a charitable foundation with their name on it that raises funds to give to causes they are passionate about. These efforts aren't as well publicized as the achievements inside the arena, but the impact their service creates can last for generations.

You may think that if you don't come from an inspiring or prosperous legacy there's nothing to carry forward. Even if there wasn't a legacy left for you, you get to create one.

So, what can the world expect from you? How are you going to serve and impact those around you, and where will you show up best? Rather than settle for the title of "former athlete," step into a new identity and responsibility. Bring everything you are becoming into this new arena.

We are waiting for you.

Stick Your Hand in the Fire

- What makes you come alive?
- What is life expecting of you?
- Will you accept the responsibility of striving to meet those expectations?
- How can you bring hope to others?
- What's a small way you can display courage today?
- Who are the people or the ideas that need you the most?
- What do you want to be remembered for?

"Many people die at twenty-five and aren't buried until they are seventy-five."

—Benjamin Franklin

Conclusion

SEE THE LIGHT

My son Blake likes to hang out on the lower level of our house. We call it the "Highlight Lounge." He finishes each day lying in the dark watching whatever game or games are on TV that particular night. I usually head down to hang out with him for a bit before it's time to head to bed. We don't talk all that much because we are both engrossed in watching, studying, and enjoying the action.

Recently on a random Tuesday night, as we flipped back and forth between the NHL and NBA playoff games, my son broke the long silence with these words: "I love sports." I couldn't help but smile. I knew exactly what he was feeling. I responded by saying that one of the best things about sports is that you can enjoy them throughout your entire life. There's no end to it. Sports will always be there for you.

Although there's always an end to every athlete's career, the connection to sports can live forever, as a fan, as a father, and as a former athlete. You can know with certainty that your relationship to sports doesn't stop when you walk out of that arena. Sports won't abandon you because you don't play anymore. Blake's three words made me realize that sports run alongside you throughout the rest of your life, encouraging you and reminding you of why you stepped into the arena in the first place. Not to mention how it can make you smile when you know you've passed on the love to another who is only beginning his life-long love affair with sports.

What does it mean when your love for something spans decades and only gets stronger over time, as you see the ways its meaning transforms and evolves?

The next play. The next game. The next season. The next opportunity. As competitive athletes, we are always looking forward to what's next. We want another chance, either to redeem a loss or duplicate the euphoria of a triumph. Especially in the agony of defeat, when the clock has expired or the buzzer has sounded for the last time, you know how disappointing it can be to have come up on the losing end of the contest. But with that feeling of frustration comes a glimmer of hope and optimism that there will be a next time. And when you emerged from a game victorious, you couldn't stop there. You wanted that feeling again. That's why Kobe, Brady, and Tiger didn't quit or retire after their first title. They wanted another. And another.

You also knew when the play, the game, or the season was over. By way of the whistle or the zeros on the scoreboard or the number of scheduled games in the season, you knew when the end was upon you. You knew who won and who lost. Even with the end of your career, you could see the end, even when you didn't want to. You could always see the finish line.

In the quest to find the meaning in your life on the outside, there is no finish line. There won't be a ceremony that ends with a medal hanging around your neck. Of course, there will be successes and accomplishments that bring you pride and recognition. And there will also be times when difficulties seem unbearable to the point that you wonder what it's all for.

But no one can tell you that you can't play this game because there aren't enough open spots. It's a game only you can play. No one can tell you to turn in your jersey or that you're not good enough.

And the end only comes when you run out of breath. There will be meaningful moments of all sizes. Victories and defeats.

Through it all, remember one thing. You are not alone. You don't have to suffer in silence. Like the other players and teammates that you shared the arena with, there are other athletes who share your struggles and the urge to find their F.I.R.E. again, find victory again. You are not alone in your frustration over losing something so central to who you were. You're not alone in your feelings of overwhelm and uncertainty. You are not the only athlete wondering who you are now without the labels.

You are also not alone in your desire to find your place in this new world. You are not alone in the nagging feeling there is more that awaits you than a life of paying the bills and living for the weekend. You are not alone in believing that you are capable of having a big impact on the world. You are not alone in your conviction and your unshakable determination to reach your full potential. The best of you is still to come.

In the time since I last laced up my cleats and threw on my helmet, I've failed time and time again. I've failed to ask for help when I could've used it. I've failed to make connections with others who would have enriched my life and become great friends. I've failed to properly thank those who selflessly helped me achieve my athletic dreams.

You will fail at times too. The arena you are stepping into will look and feel different from the one you're used to. There will be mistakes and disappointments, failed relationships, and opportunities missed. In order to live the life you are capable of, you will be tested and surprised. You will be awarded and questioned. Your hands may get a little bloody, your face a little dusty, and your body a little sweaty. But you already know a thing or two about that, don't you? Failure is sometimes the result of daring greatly. The road to victory is paved with failures.

But change is possible. Not only possible but required. Yet there can be no change without the knowledge of where you are and where you want to go. You'll need some well-placed intentions to guide you through your metamorphosis. There also can be no change without the actions that, if avoided, allow time to slip through your fingers. Finally, change will require the focus that separates the good from the great.

What you do with your life matters. It *means something*. Your relationships matter. Who you choose to spend time with matters. And the people that love you matter. The causes you undertake matter. The passion you bring to your life matters. How you handle what happens to you matters. Most importantly, how you choose to view the world and yourself in it matters.

You are built for this. So step into this new arena with your chin up and your fists clenched. Attack your days with defiance. Be unwilling to settle for less than anything but a life of significance. Don't be tempted by the comfort and complacency that you see all around you. Sidestep the status quo. Strive valiantly.

The athlete chapter of your life wasn't the climax, but instead the genesis. It was the beginning, an introduction. Time now to turn the page because a bold new chapter is on the rise. Your time inside the arena was a training ground, an internship of sorts. It was a gift that the universe bestowed on you just to see what you'd do with it once it came to a conclusion. So what *will* you do with it?

Victory awaits.

TIME OUT!

Thank you, fellow athlete, for picking up this book. I hope you found it helpful in your journey.

Before you go, I would really appreciate your feedback and would love to hear what you took away from this book.

I need your input to make the next version and my future books better.

Would you please take two minutes to leave an honest review on Amazon letting me know your thoughts?

bit.ly/VOTA_book_review

Many thanks,
Bill Burke

ABOUT THE AUTHOR

Bill Burke is a husband, father, and a Spartan. He is also a former Division 1 quarterback who played at Michigan State for the legendary coach Nick Saban. During his playing career, he contributed to victories in some of the biggest arenas in the country and helped the Spartans finish his senior year ranked #7 in the country. He is now dedicated to helping athletes with their transition to life outside of the athletic arena as well as reaching their full potential in their careers, relationships, and personal development. He currently lives in Michigan with his wife and their two children.

REFERENCES

Chapter 1

"The Man in the Arena.", The Theodore Roosevelt Center, www.theodorerooseveltcenter.org/Learn-About-TR/TR-Encyclopedia/Culture-and-Society/Man-in-the-Arena.aspx

Goldman, Robert, and Stephen Papson. *Nike Culture: The Sign of the Swoosh*. London Sage, 2004.

Scott, Nate. "Tiger Woods Hugs Son in Nearly Same Spot He Hugged His Dad after First Masters Win." *USA Today*, Gannett Satellite Information Network, 14 Apr. 2019, ftw.usatoday.com/2019/04/tiger-woods-masters-win-son-hug.

Sullivan, Paul. "Chicago Cubs Win World Series Championship with 8-7 Victory over Cleveland Indians." *Chicagotribune.com*, Chicago Tribune, 17 Nov. 2017, www.chicagotribune.com/sports/cubs/ct-cubs-win-world-series-sullivan-spt-1103-20161102-story.html.

Chapter 3

"About." *Inky Johnson*, www.inkyjohnson.com/about.

Cherry, Kendra. "Sigmund Freud's Theories and Legacy in Psychology." *Verywell Mind*, www.verywellmind.com/sigmund-freud-his-life-work-and-theories-2795860

Mcleod, Saul. "Sigmund Freud: Biography, Theories and Contribution to Psychology." *Simply Psychology*, 16 July 2023, www.simplypsychology.org/Sigmund-Freud.html.

Schaffner, Anna Katharina. "How to Escape the Hedonic Treadmill and Be Happier." *PositivePsychology.com*, 3 Oct. 2023, http://positivepsychology.com/hedonic-treadmill/

The Breakfast Club. Directed by John Hughes, Universal Pictures, 1985.

Frankl, Viktor. *Man's Search for Meaning: An Introduction to Logotherapy*. United Kingdom, Beacon Press, 1992.

Benjamin, Kathy. "The Real Reason These Great Athletes Quit Their Sports." *Grunge*, 13 May 2019, www.grunge.com/152737/the-real-reason-these-great- athletes-quit-their-sports/.

Part 2 Intro

"Mark Cuban." *Wikipedia*, Wikimedia Foundation, 22 Oct. 2023, en.wikipedia.org/wiki/Mark_Cuban.

Chapter 4

Fear of Failure Elon Musk https://www.visualcapitalist.com/elon-musk-long-list-failures/

Chapter 6

"Bookworms Live Longer." *Findings*, Yale Alumni Magazine, yalealumnimagazine.org/articles/4377-bookworms- live-longer.

Carnegie, Dale. *How To Win Friends and Influence People*. United States, Simon & Schuster, 2010.

Cherry, Kendra. "What Is Neuroplasticity?" *Verywell Mind*, 8 Nov. 2022, www.verywellmind.com/what-is-brain-plasticity-2794886.

Part 3 Intro-

"Air Traffic by the Numbers | Federal Aviation Administration." *Faa.gov*, 31 Aug. 2022, www.faa.gov/air_traffic/by_the_numbers.

Deiss, Heather. "NASA - the Wright Brothers' Story." *Www.nasa.gov*, 1 Dec. 2003, www.nasa.gov/audience/foreducators/k-4/features/F_Wright_Brothers_Story.html.

"The Wright Brothers." *Activity Village*, www.activityvillage.co.uk/the-wright-brothers.

Chapter 7

"Natural Resources at a Glance." *Www.michigan.gov*, www.michigan.gov/dnr/about/natural-resources-at-a-glance.

"Michigan." *Wikipedia*, Wikimedia Foundation, 3 Feb. 2019, en.wikipedia.org/wiki/Michigan.

"Chicago Yacht Club Race to Mackinac Presented by Wintrust." *Cycracetomackinac.com*, cycracetomackinac.com/about/race-history.

Bruce, Kalen. "The Power (and the Myths) of Written Goals." *MoneyMiniBlog*, 19 Nov. 2015, http://moneyminiblog.com/goal-setting/power-myths-written-goals/

Chapter 8

Kennedy, Robert F., Jr. "JFK's Vision of Peace." *Rolling Stone*, 20 Nov. 2013, www.rollingstone.com/politics/politics-news/john-f-kennedys-vision-of-peace-109020/.

"How Many Decisions Do We Make Each Day?" *Psychology Today*, www.psychologytoday.com/au/blog/stretching-theory/201809/how-many-decisions-do-we-make-each-day.

"Michael Phelps." *Wikipedia*, Wikimedia Foundation, 14 Dec. 2018, en.wikipedia.org/wiki/Michael_Phelps.

Perrett, Scott Davis, Connor. "Kobe Bryant's Work Ethic Was Unmatched, Here Are 24 Examples." *Business Insider*, www.businessinsider.com/kobe-bryant-insane-work-ethic-

2013-8?op=1#he-once-played-left-handed-because-he-injured-his-right-shoulder-6

"Can Sharks Swim Backwards?" *WorldAtlas*, 2 Feb. 2018, www.worldatlas.com/articles/can-sharks-swim-backwards.html.

Chapter 9

Sharapova, Maria, and Rich Cohen. *Unstoppable : My Life so Far.* New York, Sarah Crichton Books, Farrar, Straus And Giroux, 2017.

"The Marshmallow Test: Delayed Gratification in Children." *ThoughtCo*, 2019, www.thoughtco.com/the-marshmallow-test-4707284.

Part 4 Intro

"Buffalo Story | Overcoming Adversity | Building Resilience." *Rory Vaden Official Site*, www.roryvaden.com/blog-posts/buffalo-story-overcoming-adversity-building-resilience.

Chapter 10

"Grand Canyon." *HISTORY*, 2 Dec. 2009, www.history.com/topics/landmarks/grand-canyon

"Grand Canyon Rim-To-Rim Hike: Planning Guide and Checklist." *Earth Trekkers*, 16 June 2019, www.earthtrekkers.com/grand-canyon-rim-to-rim-hike-planning-guide/

"Memento Mori." *Wikipedia*, Wikimedia Foundation, 16 Nov. 2019, en.wikipedia.org/wiki/Memento_mori

Chapter 11

"What Is Gratitude?" *Gratefulness.org*, gratefulness.org/resource/what-is-gratitude-2/.

Mills, Paul J., et al. "The Role of Gratitude in Spiritual Well-Being in Asymptomatic Heart Failure Patients." *Spirituality in Clinical Practice*, vol. 2, no. 1, Mar. 2015, pp. 5–17, www.ncbi.nlm.nih.gov/pmc/articles/PMC4507265/, https://doi.org/10.1037/scp0000050

Kyeong, Sunghyon, et al. "Effects of Gratitude Meditation on Neural Network Functional Connectivity and Brain-Heart Coupling." *Scientific Reports*, vol. 7, no. 1, 11 July 2017, https://doi.org/10.1038/s41598-017-05520-9.

Kristin Layous, et al. (2017). "Feeling left out but affirmed: Protecting against the negative effects of low belonging in college." Journal of Experimental Social Psychology, Volume 69, 227-231

Ranganathan, Vinoth K, et al. "From Mental Power to Muscle Power--Gaining Strength by Using the Mind." *Neuropsychologia*, vol. 42, no. 7, 2004, pp. 944–56, www.ncbi.nlm.nih.gov/pubmed/14998709, https://doi.org/10.1016/j.neuropsychologia.2003.11.018.

Chapter 12

"Youghiogheny River's Deadly Dimple Rock Will Be Left Undisturbed." *Pittsburgh Post-Gazette*, www.post-gazette.com/local/2006/04/05/Youghiogheny-River-s-deadly-Dimple-Rock-will-be-left-undisturbed/stories/200604050261

The Shawshank Redemption. Directed by Frank Darabont, Castle Rock Entertainment, 1994.

Burg, Bob, and John David Mann. *The Go-Giver Leader : A Little Story about What Matters Most in Business.* New York, New York, Portfolio/Penguin, 2016.

Made in the USA
Las Vegas, NV
12 March 2025